The U.S. Military

D1111674

This book provides a basic guide to the U.S. military and will raise questions for further discussion by students and other curious readers.

The U.S. Military: A basic introduction provides an accessible starting-point for those with a limited knowledge of this institution. Covering a wide range of subject matter, and ending with an extensive list of suggested resources to aid individual study and research, the text is divided into the following chapters:

- The A, B, Cs
- Strategy and Doctrine
- The Military in Action
- Weapons and Capabilities
- The Budget

This book will be of great interest to students of the U.S. military, U.S. politics, defense studies, and peace and conflict studies, and of much relevance to journalists, NGO staff, and diplomats.

Judith Hicks Stiehm is Professor of Political Science at Florida International University. She is author of several books on the military and recently served as Distinguished Visiting Professor at the U.S. Air Force Academy.

Cass Military Studies

Rose Mary Sheldon, *Intelligence Activities in Ancient Rome: Trust in the Gods, But Verify*

Isabelle Duyvesteyn, *Clausewitz and African War: Politics and Strategy in Liberia and Somalia*

Michael Cohen, *Strategy and Politics in the Middle East, 1954–60: Defending the Northern Tier*

Edward George, *The Cuban Intervention in Angola, 1965–1991: From Che Guevara to Cuito Cuanavale*

Stanley Carpenter, *Military Leadership in the British Civil Wars, 1642–1651: 'The Genius of this Age'*

Ze'ev Drory, *Israel's Reprisal Policy, 1953–1956: The Dynamics of Military Retaliation*

Enver Redzic, *Bosnia and Herzegovina in the Second World War*

Frederick Kagan and Christian Kubik (eds), *Leaders in War: West Point Remembers the 1991 Gulf War*

John Dunn, *Khedive Ismail's Army*

Amadeo Watkins, *Yugoslav Military Industry 1918–1991*

John Williams, *Corporal Hitler and the Great War 1914–1918: The List Regiment*

Brian Murphy, *Rostóv in the Russian Civil War, 1917–1920: The Key to Victory*

Jake Blood, *The Tet Effect, Intelligence and the Public Perception of War*

Sam C. Sarkesian and Robert E. Connor, Jr. (eds), *The US Military Profession into the 21st Century: War, Peace and Politics*

Hans Born, Marina Caparini, Karl Haltiner and Jürgen Kuhlmann (eds), *Civil–Military Relations in Europe: Learning from Crisis and Institutional Change*

Andrew Mumford, *The Counter-Insurgency Myth: The British Experience of Irregular Warfare*

Sven Biscop and Jo Coelmont, *Europe, Strategy and Armed Forces: Towards Military Convergence*

Daniel P. McDonald and Kizzy M. Parks (eds), *Managing Diversity in the Military: The Value of Inclusion in a Culture of Uniformity*

Judith Hicks Stiehm, *The U.S. Military: A basic introduction*

The U.S. Military
A basic introduction

Judith Hicks Stiehm

LONDON AND NEW YORK

First published 2012
by Routledge
2 Park Square, Milton Park, Abingdon, Oxon, OX14 4RN

Simultaneously published in the USA and Canada
by Routledge
711 Third Avenue, New York, NY 10017

*Routledge is an imprint of the Taylor & Francis Group, an informa
business*

British Library Cataloguing in Publication Data
A catalogue record for this book is available from the British Library

Library of Congress Cataloging-in-Publication Data
Stiehm, Judith.
The US military : a basic introduction / Judith Hicks Stiehm.
p. cm.
Includes bibliographical references and index.
1. United States—Armed Forces. 2. United States—Military policy.
I. Title.
UA23.S689 2012
355.00973—dc23
2011033898

ISBN13: 978–0–415–78214–2 (hbk)
ISBN13: 978–0–415–78215–9 (pbk)
ISBN13: 978–0–203–12800–8 (ebk)

Typeset in Times New Roman by Prepress Projects Ltd, Perth, UK

Contents

Figures

Tables

Acknowledgments

Any errors which appear in this handbook are mine. Others were avoided by the wise counsel of many individuals including Kathleen Mahoney-Norris, David Burbach, Jennifer Lamm, Steven Biddle, Michael O'Hanlon, Michael Gleason, David McCone, Wil Scott, Larry Korb, Lory Manning, and Lytton Cosens.

Abbreviations

ACLU	American Civil Liberties Union
AEI	American Enterprise Institute
AFPS	Armed Forces Press Service
AFSC	Air Force Specialty Code
AID	Agency for International Development
AOC	Area of Concentration Code
ASVAB	Armed Services Vocational Aptitude Battery
BCT	Basic Combat Training
BRAC	Base Realignment and Closure Commission
CBO	Congressional Budget Office
CDI	Center for Defense Information
CIA	Central Intelligence Agency
CMF	Career Management Field
CNA	Center for Naval Analysis
CONPLANS	concept plans
CSIS	Center for Strategic and International Studies
DARPA	Defense Advanced Research Program Agency
DEA	Drug Enforcement Agency
DIA	Defense Intelligence Agency
DOD	Department of Defense
FA	Functional Area Code
FAS	Federation of American Scientists
FBI	Federal Bureau of Investigation
FMTV	Family of Medium Tracked Vehicles
FYDP	Future Years Defense Program

GDP	gross domestic product
HEMTT	Heavy Expanded Mobility Tactical Truck
HET	Heavy Equipment Transporter
HMMWV	High Mobility Multipurpose Wheeled Vehicle
HUMINT	human intelligence
ICBM	Inter-Continental Ballistic Missile
JAG	Judge Advocate
JCS	Joint Chiefs of Staff
LIC	Low Intensity Conflict
MAGTF	Marine Air–Ground Task Force
MARO	Mass Atrocity Response Operations
MEF	Marine Expeditionary Force
MEU	Marine Expeditionary Unit
MNF-I	Multi National Force Iraq
MOOTW	Military Operations Other Than War
MOSC	Military Occupational Specialty Code
NATO	North Atlantic Treaty Organization
NCA	National Command Authority
NCO	noncommissioned officer
NGA	National Geospatial Intelligence Agency
NGO	nongovernmental organization
NJP	non-judicial punishment
NMS	National Military Strategy
NOOCS	Naval Officer Occupational Classification System
NPT	Non Proliferation Treaty
NRO	National Reconnaissance Office
NSA	National Security Agency
NSS	National Security Strategy
OMB	Office of Management and the Budget
OPPLANS	operation plans
OSD	Office of the Secretary of Defense
PLS	Palletized Load System
PMC	private military company
PME	Professional Military Education
POM	program objective memoranda
POW	prisoner of war
PPBE	Planning Programming Budgeting and Execution

PRT	Provincial Reconstruction Teams
QDR	Quadrennial Defense Review
ROE	Rules of Engagement
RPV	Remotely Piloted Vehicle
SAW	Squad Automatic Weapon
SIPRI	Stockholm International Peace Research Institute
SLBM	Submarine Launched Ballistic Missile
SOFA	status of forces agreement
START	Strategic Arms Reduction Treaty
STRACT	strategically ready and combat tough
TOW	Tube launched, Optically Guided, Wire command data link
TRADOC	Training and Doctrine Command
UAV	Unmanned Aerial Vehicle
UCMJ	Uniform Code of Military Justice
USMC	United States Marine Corps
WMD	weapons of mass destruction
WOMOS	Warrant Officer Military Occupational Specialty

1 Introduction

For most Americans the words of the Declaration of Independence are something of a mantra. Providing "life, liberty and the pursuit of happiness" is seen as the "self evident" purpose of government, and Americans generally honor the assertion that "all men are created equal." The military is composed of individuals who may be committed to these principles, but they have, nevertheless, chosen to join an organization where they may be asked to kill people and, perhaps, asked to sacrifice their lives. They serve in a rule-bound organization in which "liberty" is a time out for which one gets a pass, not the everyday experience. Also, although happiness means different things to different people, for most there is usually some association with pleasure based on material and/or physical well being. For the military it is likely to be connected to service and/or to honor. Further, every individual's uniform clearly marks his or her location in a hierarchy. At a glance one can determine if someone is a subordinate, and just how subordinate, and, conversely, if an individual is one's superior.

In some countries the military *is* the government. In others it may have an informal veto. In some it runs businesses to fund itself. In the United States, civilian control is the rule. An elected official is the military's Commander in Chief and the military depends on an elected legislature to provide it with resources. In addition, civilians make rules about the military and the U.S. Senate must approve senior promotions. Because those commanding the nation's arsenal take their orders from elected officials, it is important that those officials, the citizens who elect them, and U.S. allies and enemies understand the nature of the U.S. military – how it operates, what it can and cannot do, its expectations, its values.

Since World War II the U.S. has had a large, standing, peacetime military. The nation's founders generally opposed such a force, but in the last sixty years few have argued against it. The only postwar presidents to publicly question much about the military were West Point graduate and former five star general, Dwight D. Eisenhower, Jimmy Carter, an Annapolis graduate, and Missouri's Harry Truman, who famously fired a five star general, Douglas MacArthur. Congress has also been relatively uncritical of the military, and, importantly, public opinion research shows that the military is one of the nation's most respected institutions. Citizens debate taxes and education and abortion and health insurance with passion, but they rarely debate issues related to the military – at least until the United States has been in a particular war for a long time. Then calls begin to "get out."

My experience has been that few of my students, or even my colleagues, have a lot of information about the military. Even those who take political debate and voting seriously tend *not* to be informed about the military. They may know that the Constitution makes the President the Commander in Chief and that Congress has the responsibility for declaring war even though it has not done so since World War II.[1] For the most part, though, they, and most citizens, give elected officials a blank check when it comes to that expensive and lethal institution known as the U.S. military.

The purpose of this book is simple. It is to provide accessible, useful information about the U.S. military. Discussion about how it might be or should be used will be deferred. The goal is only to provide an account free of fog and excessive numbers, which will enable readers to participate intelligently in debate about a military that possesses unmatched power and reach.

The first section, "The A, B, Cs," briefly describes the services and their missions. The differences between Regular, Reserve and National Guard forces are explained, and demographic data show just who is serving in the military. Next, some of the differences between civilian and military culture are illustrated through a discussion of military customs and courtesies and military lifestyle and culture. The constitutional and legal bases for the military and the kind of control exercised by the three branches of government, executive, legislative and judicial, are outlined and the military justice system is discussed. Visuals of military insignia and uniforms are presented. This is followed by a description of the structure of the unified commands, and the organization of the separate services. Finally, the range of military specialties and data on compensation and benefits for active duty troops and for veterans are described.

The second section explores strategy and doctrine. There is a National Security Strategy, which cites diplomacy, economic measures, and military force as the means to achieving national goals. There is a substrategy, a National Defense Strategy, which assesses the threat environment and evaluates the nation's "capabilities" to respond. In considering military analyses one might remember Samuel P. Huntington's admonition that the military's tendency, and perhaps its job, is to consider worst case scenarios. That view has been described as "realist," but, realistically, few governments act and few citizens lead their lives based on worst case possibilities. Thus, the degree of risk to be assumed is an important question to address in determining the size and nature of any military.

Military analyses examine strategy, operations and tactics. This involves setting the military goal and establishing the variety of means needed to achieve it. Senior officers develop the strategy and plan operations. Tactics, which are executed by small units, are largely prescribed. Much about operations and especially tactics is learned as doctrine and inscribed in manuals. The point of doctrine and the manuals is to make it possible to act quickly and with coordination. The problem is, as the military always acknowledges, that things *never* go according to plan. Thus, the assumptions and activities summarized in this section are, inevitably, adapted once action begins.

The third section focuses on the military in action. Recruitment, training and education are summarized. The military spends a lot of time on planning for a range of contingencies and a lot of money on research, much of it allocated to civilian investigators in universities and research centers. The planning process and the range of research topics is detailed. The collection and analysis of intelligence are important to both functions. Next, the military's diplomatic efforts will be examined. This includes outreach to civilians and local communities, representations to Congress and the executive, and sometimes awkward dealings with the media. It also includes a wide variety of military-to-military contacts. These include training and advising militaries of other countries. The location of U.S. bases in foreign countries will be discussed in this section.

The military is used in many ways. It can deliver humanitarian aid or intervene in a domestic conflict or even in a conflict between countries. It can conduct surveillance, engage in peacekeeping, stability, counterterrorist and counterinsurgency operations, and it can deter conflict by demonstrating commitment to protect an ally. Although conducting war is the military's unique function, the one it recruits, trains, educates, researches, and plans for, it does so with the belief that preparation is the best way to avoid actually going to war.[2]

Readers may be tempted to skip the section on weapons and capabilities. Do not.

It is important to know what the U.S. military can do, what it costs, and how its weapons relate to strategy. Weaponry is not "too complicated" and "willful ignorance" is not acceptable. Further, one should understand the consequences of a weapon's use. Knowing whether a weapon can discriminate between an enemy and a child is important not only for legal and ethical reasons, but also because poor discrimination affects the effectiveness of an operation. Consideration will be given here to military capabilities, for example transportation capacity, and to "force protection." Both play an important part in the designing of strategy and in the choice of weapons.

Readers are also admonished not to skip the section on the budget. Many know that the United States spends about as much on its military as all other countries combined. Many also know that even setting aside the Iraq and Afghanistan wars the U.S. military budget has been increasing. The procedures and numbers may be daunting, but money is always important. This section outlines budgeting procedures and their recent results. It includes money spent for military purposes through contracting and outsourcing. It notes the profit made by sales of weapons to other countries and suggests the possible amount and purposes of the "black budget."[3]

This volume will not explore policy issues in detail. Its purpose is only to describe the basic nature of the U.S. military and, thus, to lay the groundwork for debate about its "proper" nature and use. Some issues involve defining the national interest, exercising and respecting sovereignty, the "duty to protect," the level of risk to be assumed, and the requirements of international law. Conscription is currently off the agenda but relevant. Although active duty officers are supposed to be nonpolitical, some are now asking what this means in practice, and also what should be expected of retired officers.

Finally, this volume will assist readers in doing their own research by listing a sampling of research organizations, websites, periodicals, books and even films which can contribute to further understanding.

2 The A, B, Cs

The services and their missions

There are five military services. The primary mission of one, the Coast Guard, is to protect the coastline, although it does have some missions abroad. It also has rescue and law enforcement responsibilities. The Coast Guard has had different governmental homes. Currently it is part of the Department of Homeland Security, although in time of war it has been placed under the Navy. The focus here, however, is on the four military services located in the Department of Defense (DOD) and housed in the Pentagon. Thus, the Coast Guard will not be discussed further. As will be seen, the missions and cultures of the four DOD services are quite different.

Originally there was only a Department of War. The Navy acquired its own department and civilian secretary in 1798. Until 1947 the secretaries of both departments had a seat in the President's cabinet. Now there are three civilian service secretaries, Army, Navy and Air Force, each of whom reports to the Secretary of Defense. Only he, thus far, is a member of today's cabinet.

The Army's mission is land combat – for almost a century and a half that combat has occurred abroad. The Navy's "turf" is on and under the high seas, the U.S. littoral and the littoral of some other countries as well. Both the Army and the Navy have fleets of planes. Nevertheless, the Air Force emerged from the Army as a separate service after World War II. It has a special responsibility for space as well as air. Then there is the Marine Corps. The Marines are a part of the Department of the Navy. Some might call them the Navy's Army. Their special role has been to fight from ship to shore, to be amphibious. They are different from the other services because they are overwhelmingly a combat force. Their support, for example medical care, is provided by the Navy. Again, the Marines are separate from the Navy, but not from the Department of the Navy. They do have their own member of the Joint Chiefs of Staff (JCS) and a small and new war college. They do not have a separate service academy.

The military's unique mission is combat: fighting and winning the nation's wars. However, an individual's chance of participating in combat varies by service and specialty. Fewer than 5 percent of Air Force personnel are expected to be in combat and at risk. These include the crews of combat planes (mostly officers) and members of Air Force Special Forces units (mostly enlisted personnel). Other services some-times call the Air Force the civilian service and harrumph about its purportedly easy lifestyle and its public relations successes such as movies showing "right stuff" officers and its always popular air shows. The Air Force has a significant constituency in the corporate world. This includes officials and stock holders in corporations that build its aircraft as well as the many workers who produce them. To some degree that constituency is concentrated where there are major plants. However, it is also well distributed because aircraft components, and also the weapons and equipment of the other services, are produced throughout the country. This means many members of Congress have constituents whose jobs are tied to the defense budget.

Even though aircraft deployed from the Navy's carriers are playing an important role in land combat, the Navy has not engaged in signifi-cant naval combat since World War II. North Korea, Vietnam, and Iraq do not have much in the way of a navy, and Afghanistan has not even contemplated one. One's risk in the Navy, then, has been relatively low even though the Navy patrols much of the world's oceans. This has not been true for the Army or more especially for the Marines. Both engage in land combat. However, the Army has a long "tooth to tail" and as many as two-thirds of its personnel are in support rather than combat specialties.[1] Still, it is a large service and many soldiers do fight. Those most at risk are enlisted troops and junior officers. The Marines, the smallest service, describe themselves as "warriors" and assert "every man a rifleman." Because the Navy provides its support, its members are the ones most likely to see combat, to fight, to act out the images of combat offered up by Hollywood. Some have described the Marines as military fundamentalists. They concentrate on doing what only the military does – fight.

Carl Builder has described the differences between the services as "profound, pervasive, and persistent."[2] Although his account is dated and does not include the Marines as a separate service, it continues to ring true. He describes the Air Force as focused on the newest in technology and enthralled by its aircraft. He notes its connections with corporate America, its self-confident and effective lobbying with Congress, and its "modernity" as symbolized by the architecture of its academy, in particular, its chapel, in Colorado Springs, Colorado. The Navy, he suggests, honors tradition more than the other services. Style means something in the Navy, and there is a certain toleration of the eccentric or individual, perhaps related to the days when the commander of a ship at sea was out of touch and had to exercise judgment. In the Navy commanding a ship is all and the kind of ship matters. Thus, the submariners have a community of their own, and commanding an aircraft carrier (there are about a dozen in active service) is a very different assignment from commanding a destroyer. Ship to shore rotations and a mission of power projection give the Navy a special character. Builder describes the Army, the largest service, as the loyal Boy Scout, as a service deeply committed to service but a service without flair. Its responsibilities are not dramatic; its weapons are not sexy; even its uniforms are dull.[3] (The Marines have the best dress uniforms, whereas Navy enlisted have the best service dress uniforms, the so-called crackerjacks.) The Army has long-standing traditions and documents its history in a way the other services do not. It also has a reputation for doing high-quality research about itself and making it available to the public even when the results are not as hoped.

There is no question but that the services compete with each other. This can be positive when it leads to innovation, but negative when it interferes with joint operations. To enhance cooperation between the services the DOD developed a series of "joint" policies and even a Joint Forces Unified Combatant Command.[4] What most service members do share is a sense of patriotism that goes beyond that of many civilians. They also share a sense of how they are different from civilians. Civilians may think of the soldier, sailor, airman and marine as "different," but it probably does not occur to civilians that service personnel see them as different too. To those who wear uniforms, civilians may seem ill-disciplined, individualistic, self-centered, mercenary, more inclined to words than action, as wanting the military to do the dirty work for them, and as willfully ignorant of what the military does, and, in particular, of what those who fight go through. Samuel P. Huntington's description of the military as a profession and of the "military mind" is accepted as true enough to be regularly cited (or disputed).[5] There may be something like a civilian mind as well.[6]

Regular, Reserve, and National Guard forces

Regular members of the military are on active duty. However, so are many members of the National Guard and the Reserves. The Guard and Reserves together are roughly half as large as the Regular military and require some explanation.

A (federal) National Guard Bureau establishes policies, especially policies related to training, and provides the state units with equipment and funding. However, the Guard is organized by and based in the fifty states (and in the territories). Its origin was the various state militias dating to the founding of the country. Individuals can join the National Guard directly, although many have had prior military experience. Those without prior service go through eight weeks of basic training and some further training in a specialty. Well described as citizen-soldiers, members of the Guard have civilian lives, responsibilities and occupations. If they are mobilized, their employers are required to reinstate them on completion of their tour. Sometimes called "weekend warriors," personnel typically train one weekend a month and for several weeks in the summer. There is an Army National Guard of more than 350,000 and an Air National Guard of more than 100,000, but no Navy or Marine National Guard.[7]

State governors command Guard units and can activate them for assistance in emergencies and disasters. Unlike Regular military forces, the National Guard can be used to enforce domestic law. At the beginning of the twentieth century, legislation was passed to make Guard units a reserve for the Army and provision was made to federalize the Guard during war or emergency. Many Guard units were federalized and mobilized in World Wars I and II and during the Korean War. The Guard was *not* mobilized during the Vietnam War and some, including George W. Bush, may have joined it to stay out of the war.

Draftees were available to fight the Vietnam War. However, when the draft ended in 1973 reserve forces became more important, and a "Total Force Policy" was enunciated, which defines all Regular and Guard *and* Reserve military organizations as part of a single force.[8] In the past the appropriate governor had to consent to the federalizing of a state's troops. However, in 1987 the Montgomery Amendment to the National Defense Authorization Act stated that a governor could not withhold consent to call Guard troops to active duty, even for duty outside the United States. Challenged in court, the provision was upheld by the Supreme Court in Perpich v. Department of Defense in 1990.

Today National Guard units are regularly sent abroad and into combat. In fact, in January 2010 there were 142,000 National Guard and Reserve troops on active duty. There have been 700,000 mobilizations of these reserves since the beginning of the Iraq War; indeed, many "civilian warriors" have been deployed more than once.[9]

Again, the Guard is a "reserve component" of the military that is being used regularly. So are the 350,000 to 400,000 members of the Army Reserve, the Naval Reserve, the Marine Corps Reserve, and the Air Force Reserve. Individuals may join the Reserves directly but many members of the Reserves have served previously. Indeed, when individuals enlist in the military they typically incur an eight-year obligation with a specified amount of time, two to six years, on active duty with the remainder to be served in the Reserves.

Like members of the Guard, reservists are civilians with a military obligation who typically train one weekend a month and two weeks a year. Some are in the Ready Reserve (as are all Guard members) and are called to duty if the United States is engaged in a major or sustained conflict. Other Reservists are in the Standby Reserve, or the Retired Reserve.[10] There are also members of the Individual Ready Reserve who do not drill. Reservists may be activated as units or as individuals.

It is important to realize that, at least at present, when the United States fights a war, many of the uniformed troops may think of themselves as civilians called to temporary duty:[11] In contrast, members of the Regular force include men and women at senior officer and senior enlisted ranks who may think of themselves as professionals. A large portion of the junior Regular troops, though, may plan to serve only a short time and may have a variety of motivations. Some join to serve. Some see the military as an opportunity to build a career or to acquire a nest egg or educational benefits. Further, any combat zone is now full of civilians under contract to perform duties once carried out by the military. Indeed, in the recent past there were more DOD contracted workers in Afghanistan than military forces![12] Contracted civilians do not just do kitchen duty and deliver mail; some carry weapons and interrogate prisoners. Some are highly paid former members of the U.S. military. Others are low-wage local workers or even workers brought in from a third country.

There are still other civilians working in a conflict zone, for example in humanitarian relief. This can include State Department or Agency for International Development (AID) or United Nations personnel. It can also include employees of nongovernmental organizations such as the International Red Cross and Doctors Without Borders as well as members of the media. The relationship between these various groups and the military is sometimes strained.[13]

Demographics

Part of understanding the military involves understanding who serves and who does not.[14]

The military is not representative of the U.S. population. It is obvious that it is largely composed of men and the young, but it varies from the U.S. population in other ways as well. Also, the different services have rather different demographics.

First, there are about 1.4 million active-duty military. Close to 40 percent of these are in the Army. The Navy and Air Force are under 25 percent, the Marines about 14 percent. Women are about 14 percent of the military; the Air Force has close to 20 percent women, the Marine

Corps around 6 percent. The military is young. Two thirds of personnel are under thirty and fewer than 10 percent are over forty.

Enlisted personnel are about 85 percent of the force and typically have a high school degree or a GED (General Educational Diploma).[15] Officers are about 15 percent of the total and most have a college degree. In fact, most senior officers have a graduate degree.

About 6 percent of recruits come from neighborhoods with a family median income of more than $90,000 a year. A similar percentage come from neighborhoods with family median incomes of less than $30,000 a year. The military is decidedly middle-class. One reason there are so few low-income recruits is that as many as 25 or 30 percent of young people, many of them low-income, are ineligible for lack of education or low aptitude scores. Others are ineligible because they do not meet physical standards or have criminal records.[16]

About three fourths of the military is white; 18 percent is Black, and Black troops are to some degree concentrated in the Army and the Navy. Hispanics are underrepresented in the military. They tend to concentrate in the Navy and more especially in the Marines. Recruits tend to come from the mountain states and the south, least often from the northeast. They often come from small towns, less often from large cities.

Half the enlisted force and 70 percent of officers are married. Current data also suggest that the military is more Republican and more religious than society as a whole.

Customs and courtesies

Customs and courtesies are practices which demonstrate military pride and discipline. They are formally taught to new members and one is expected to honor them. Many customs are practiced by all services and all ranks. These include such things as not publicly criticizing a military leader or a military service, not jumping the chain of command, and not offering excuses. They include treating a senior's "wish" as a command, and addressing one's senior as "sir" or "ma'am."

Each service has a creed which is known and treated seriously. They are as follows:

The Soldier's Creed

I am an American Soldier.

I am a Warrior and a member of a team. I serve the people of the United States and live the Army Values.

I will always place the mission first.

I will never accept defeat.

I will never quit.

I will never leave a fallen comrade.

I am disciplined, physically and mentally tough, trained and proficient in my warrior tasks and drills. I always maintain my arms, my equipment, and myself.

I am an expert and I am a professional.

I stand ready to deploy, engage, and destroy the enemies of the United States of America in close combat.

I am a guardian of freedom and the American way of life.

I am an American Soldier

The Airman's Creed

I am an American Airman.

I am a Warrior.

I have answered my Nation's call.

I am an American Airman.

My mission is to Fly, Fight, and Win.

I am faithful to a Proud Heritage,

A Tradition of Honor,

And a Legacy of Valor.

I am an American Airman.

Guardian of Freedom and Justice.

My Nation's Sword and Shield,

Its Sentry and Avenger.

I defend my Country with my Life.

I am an American Airman.

Wingman, Leader, Warrior.

I will never leave an Airman behind.

I will never falter,

And I will not fail.

The Sailors' Creed

I am a United States Sailor.
I will support and defend the Constitution of the United States of America and I will obey the orders of those appointed over me.
I represent the fighting spirit of the Navy and those who have gone before me to defend freedom and democracy around the world.
I proudly serve my country's Navy combat team with Honor, Courage and Commitment,
I am committed to excellence and the fair treatment of all.

The Marine Corps' creed is longer and different in tone.

My Rifle - The Creed of a United States Marine

1 This is my rifle. There are many like it, but this one is mine.
2 My rifle is my best friend. It is my life. I must master it as I must master my life.
3 My rifle, without me, is useless. Without my rifle, I am useless. I must fire my rifle true. I must shoot straighter than my enemy who is trying to kill me. I must shoot him before he shoots me. I will . . .
4 My rifle and myself know that what counts in this war is not the rounds we fire, the noise of our burst, nor the smoke we make. We know that it is the hits that count. We will hit . . .
5 My rifle is human, even as I, because it is my life. Thus. I will learn it as a brother. I will learn its weaknesses, its strength, its parts, its accessories, its sights and its barrel. I will ever guard it against the ravages of weather and damage as I will ever guard my legs, my arms, my eyes and my heart against damage. I will keep my rifle clean and ready. We will become part of each other. We will . . .
6 Before God, I swear this creed. My rifle and myself are the defenders of my country. We are the masters of our enemy. We are the saviors of my life.
7 So be it, until victory is America's and there is no enemy, but peace!

Creeds are not a matter of law, but the oath for enlistment and for the commissioning of officers are prescribed. The oath of enlistment is clear about obedience. It is:

I, _____, do solemnly swear (or affirm) that I will support and defend the Constitution of the United States against all enemies, foreign and domestic; that I will bear true faith and allegiance to the same; and that I will obey the orders of the President of the United States and the orders of the officers appointed over me, according to regulations and the Uniform Code of Military Justice. So help me God.

The 15 percent of the military who are officers have a different oath. Theirs is to the Constitution but says nothing about obedience to a superior.

I, _____, having been appointed an officer in the Army [NAVY, AIR FORCE, MARINE CORPS] of the United States, as indicated Above in the grade of _____ do solemnly swear (or affirm) that I will support and defend the Constitution of the United States against all enemies, foreign or domestic, that I will bear true faith and allegiance to the same; that I take this obligation freely, without any mental reservations or purpose of evasion; and that I will well and faithfully discharge the duties of the office upon which I am about to enter. So help me God.

The creeds and the oaths give definition to the commitment one makes when entering military service. Physicians have a Hippocratic Oath, which functions as a creed, and elected officials take an oath of office. Members of certain organizations, for example, certain churches, make a pledge of belief and/or commitment. These involve varying levels of significance to particular individuals, but the military tends to see these formal statements as important to cohesion, to commitment to the team, to the service, to something beyond oneself. In military culture individualism, a central part of American culture, gives way to acknowledgment of community, interdependence, and hierarchy.

Each service has a song. The service songs are: Air Force, "The U.S. Air Force," also known as "The Wild Blue Yonder"; Navy, "Anchors Aweigh"; Army, "The Army Goes Rolling Along" or "The Caission Song"; and Marines, "The Marine Hymn," also known as "From the Halls of Montezuma."

Courtesies involve protocol. The most important protocols involve the flag and the salute. There are a lot of flags in any military setting and there is a great deal of etiquette associated with them including a designated order of precedence, a prescribed size, the proper way to fold them and even the proper finial (head of the flagstaff).

It is important that the salute be "correctly and smartly executed." The salute is offered to an individual of rank higher than one's own from six paces away and held until it is returned.[17] Generally, it is not required while indoors or in civilian clothing, but it is required when meeting out of doors and both are in uniform, when the flag is being raised, lowered, or honored, at ceremonies such as funerals and change of command, and when certain military music is being played. The salute is required for "The National Anthem," "Hail to the Chief," "To the Colors" (played while the flag is being raised or lowered), "Reveille," "Retreat" (sundown), and "Taps." If one is not in uniform, one honors the flag by standing at attention uncovered (i.e., no hat) with right hand on one's heart. There is more (much more) such as the Navy's "manning the rails" of a ship to render honor, gun salutes and fly-overs.

Lifestyle and culture

Lifestyle and culture include the accepted, expected, shared way of life. One characteristic of military life is that one is on call 24–7. Another is that one is constantly in motion. Individuals regularly rotate locations and jobs. They get new superiors and have to learn about new subordinates committed to their care. They receive promotions and new responsibilities. They are sent to sea or given temporary duty far from home and without their families. Culture also includes traditions, ceremonies, heroes, humor, legends, mottos, language, acronyms – the kind of things anthropologists study. These must be learned, even if they do not appear in manuals or curricula, and even if some (various forms of hazing) are carefully unacknowledged.

The culture of the Regular military is basically male and youthful. Sex, cars and booze or its equivalent are said to be central to the lives of young men. Well, cars may be important to military men (and women), but, partly because recent deployments have been to Islamic countries, drinking has been curtailed, as has recreational sex. Another moderating force is the fact that the military is a family affair. In fact, a majority of active duty personnel have children. As recently as the Vietnam War, merely being married exempted one from the draft. The facts, then, are very much at odds with film or literary portrayals of the hard partying, single soldier and his buddies. Families are all important to the military. Indeed, the DOD has a Deputy Under Secretary for Military Community and Family Policy.

Some items peculiar to a service include the mottoes of Army units, for example "Airborne all the way" and the Army's "HOOAH," a loud affirmation of commitment that stands for "Heard, Understood and Acknowledged", the Marine's "Semper Fi" and "Once a Marine Always a Marine" mottoes, the Air Force's core values "Integrity First, Service before Self and Excellence in All you Do", and the Navy's "Cup of Joe" for coffee commemorating the Secretary of the Navy who banned alcohol on ships.

Legal bases

The Constitution designates the President, an elected official and almost necessarily a political partisan, as Commander in Chief. Over the years twelve generals have become President after they left the Army. These include George Washington, Andrew Jackson, Ulysses S. Grant and five others who served during the Civil War. The only former general to become President in the twentieth century was Dwight D. Eisenhower in 1952. Civilian control of the military is a central premise of the U.S. Constitution.

The authors of the Constitution deplored the notion of a "standing [peacetime] army." The theory was that, if you had a military, you would use it – perhaps to coerce citizens, perhaps to indulge in foreign adventures. For 150 years the United States maintained only a skeleton military between wars. However, since World War II the United States has maintained a large and potent military with a global reach. It could be argued that the United States was, in fact, engaged in a war (Cold) until twenty years ago and that after the Soviet Union collapsed the United States did reduce its forces by about 25 percent. However, it is also true that, almost as soon as the Soviet threat dissolved, U.S. forces undertook a number of foreign actions. These included two major wars in the Persian Gulf and one in Afghanistan. In addition, in the decade between 1989 and 1999 the United States sent troops to Panama to overthrow a government, to Bosnia, to Somalia, to Kenya, to East Timor, and to Haiti. The United States bombed Libya and Kosovo and it rescued or positioned troops for a rescue in Sierra Leone, Zaire, and Turkey. The result has been the routine use of Reserve and National Guard troops and, more recently, of contracted civilians.

The President presides over a bureaucracy of close to 700,000 civilian employees in the Department of Defense.[18] An organizational chart is provided in Figure 2.1.

The Office of the Secretary of Defense (OSD) includes a deputy secretary and something like four under secretaries, twenty deputy under secretaries and assistant secretaries, plus a set of directors, and an inspector general and a general counsel! There are seventeen agencies, and more than ten field activities. The most senior civilian positions are appointed by the President and approved by the Senate. Most of the other employees are members of the civil service; this provides continuity.

As Commander in Chief the President also presides over a military of almost 1.5 million Regular troops and half as many more Guard and Reserve troops. The Military Departments are a part of the Department of Defense and are headed by civilian Secretaries of the Army, Navy, and Air Force. These secretaries report to the Secretary of Defense and are responsible for recruiting, training, and equipping the military. As will be discussed below, two other important organizations report to the Secretary of Defense and to the President. They are the Joint Chiefs of Staff and the Unified Combatant Commands.

The Constitution specifically states that a declaration of war is the responsibility of Congress, an elected legislature. However, the last war Congress declared was World War II. There was a formal

Department of Defense

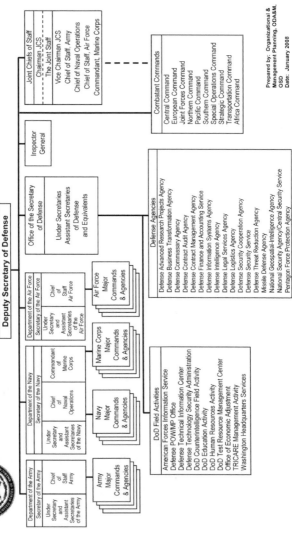

Secretary of Defense

Deputy Secretary of Defense

Department of the Army
Secretary of the Army
- Under Secretary and Assistant Secretaries of the Army
- Chief of Staff Army
- Army Major Commands & Agencies

Department of the Navy
Secretary of the Navy
- Under Secretary and Assistant Secretaries of the Navy
- Chief of Naval Operations
- Commandant of Marine Corps
- Navy Major Commands & Agencies
- Marine Corps Major Commands & Agencies

Department of the Air Force
Secretary of the Air Force
- Under Secretary and Assistant Secretaries of the Air Force
- Chief of Staff Air Force
- Air Force Major Commands & Agencies

Office of the Secretary of Defense
- Under Secretaries Assistant Secretaries of Defense and Equivalents

Inspector General

Joint Chiefs of Staff
- Chairman JCS
- The Joint Staff
- Vice Chairman JCS
- Chief of Staff, Army
- Chief of Naval Operations
- Chief of Staff, Air Force
- Commandant, Marine Corps

Combatant Commands
- Central Command
- European Command
- Joint Forces Command
- Northern Command
- Pacific Command
- Southern Command
- Special Operations Command
- Strategic Command
- Transportation Command
- Africa Command

DoD Field Activities
- American Forces Information Service
- Defense POW/MP Office
- Defense Technical Information Center
- Defense Technology Security Administration
- DoD Counterintelligence Field Activity
- DoD Education Activity
- DoD Human Resources Activity
- DoD Test Resource Management Center
- Office of Economic Adjustment
- TRICARE Management Activity
- Washington Headquarters Services

Defense Agencies
- Defense Advanced Research Projects Agency
- Defense Business Transformation Agency
- Defense Commissary Agency
- Defense Contract Audit Agency
- Defense Contract Management Agency
- Defense Finance and Accounting Service
- Defense Information Systems Agency
- Defense Intelligence Agency
- Defense Legal Services Agency
- Defense Logistics Agency
- Defense Security Cooperation Agency
- Defense Security Service
- Defense Threat Reduction Agency
- Missile Defense Agency
- National Geospatial-Intelligence Agency
- National Security Agency/Central Security Service
- Pentagon Force Protection Agency

Prepared by: Organizational & Management Planning, ODA&M, OSD
Date: January 2008

Figure 2.1 DOD organization chart. Source: www.defenselink.mil.

debate and a vote authorizing the first Gulf War, but more often Congress evades responsibility by offering a conditional or permissive resolution leaving the decision to send troops into combat to the executive.[19]

Congress has the specific responsibility for raising an Army and maintaining a Navy. It makes the rules (laws) about the military with the President or passes them over his veto. Thus, the military, an institution which reveres a chain of command, has to respond to two authorities – authorities which do not always agree. Members of the House and Senate Armed Services Committees and the House and Senate Appropriations Committees and their staffs are the primary contact between the military and the Congress. The services assign officers as liaison to the Congress and officers can be called to testify before Congressional committees. Many committee members and staff have extensive experience and knowledge about the military and play a crucial role in shaping legislation. Committee membership reflects the partisan makeup of the House and Senate; that is, the majority party always has a majority of committee members. Here is the membership of the four committees in 2011.

House Armed Services Committee and Subcommittees Chairs and Ranking Members

Armed Services Committee

- Chair Howard P. "Buck" McKeon, R-California
- Vice Chair Mac Thornberry, R-Texas, Ranking Member Adam Smith, D-Washington

Subcommittee on Tactical Air and Land Forces

- Chair Roscoe G. Bartlett, R-Maryland, Ranking Member Silvestre Reyes, D-Texas

Subcommittee on Military Personnel

- Chair Joe Wilson, R-South Carolina, Ranking Member Susan A. Davis, D-California

Subcommittee on Oversight and Investigation

• Chair Rob Whitman, R-Virginia, Ranking Member Jim Cooper, D-Tennessee

Subcommittee on Readiness

• Chair J. Randy Forbes, R-Virginia, Ranking Member Madeleine Z. Bordallo, D-Guam

Subcommittee on Seapower and Projection Forces

• Chair W. Todd Akin R-Missouri, Ranking Member Mike McIntyre, D-North Carolina

Subcommittee on Strategic Forces

• Chair Michael Turner, R-Ohio, Ranking Member Loretta Sanchez, D-California

Subcommittee on Emerging Threats and Capabilities

• Chair Mac Thornberry, R-Texas, Ranking Member James R. Langevin, D-Rhode Island

The Committee is composed of thirty-five Republicans and twenty-seven Democrats.

Membership of the Defense Subcommittee of the House Appropriations Committee

Republicans

• Chair C. W. Bill Young, Florida
• Jerry Lewis, California
• Rodney Frelinghuysen, New Jersey
• Jack Kingston, Georgia
• Kay Granger, Texas
• Ander Crenshaw, Florida
• Ken Calvert, California

- Jo Bonner, Alabama
- Tom Cole, Oklahoma

Democrats

- Norman Dicks, Washington
- Pete Visclosky, Indiana
- Jim Moran, Virginia
- Marcy Kaptur, Ohio
- Steve Rothman, New Jersey
- Maurice Hinchey, New York

Senate Armed Services Committee and Subcommittee Chairs and Ranking Members

Armed Services Committee

- Chair, Carl Levin, D-Michigan, Ranking Member John McCain, R-Arizona

Subcommittee on Airland

- Chair Joseph I. Lieberman, I-Connecticut, Ranking Member James M. Inhofe, R-Oklahoma

Subcommittee on Personnel

- Chair Jim Webb, D-Virginia, Ranking Member Lindsey Graham, R-South Carolina

Subcommittee on Readiness and Management Support

- Chair Claire McCaskill, D-Missouri, Ranking Member Kelly Ayotte, R-New Hampshire

Subcommittee on Seapower

- Chair Jack Reed, D-Rhode Island, Ranking Member Roger F. Wicker, R-Mississippi

Subcommittee on Emerging Threats and Capabilities

- Chair Kay R. Hagan, D-North Carolina, Ranking Member Rob Portman, R-Ohio

Subcommittee on Strategic Forces

- Chair Ben Nelson, D-Nebraska, Ranking Member Jeff Sessions, R-Alabama

Membership of the Defense Subcommittee of the Senate Appropriations Committee

Democrats

- Chair Daniel Inouye, Hawaii
- Patrick Leahy, Vermont
- Tom Harkin, Iowa
- Richard Durbin, Illinois
- Dianne Feinstein, California
- Barbara Mikulski, Maryland
- Herb Kohl, Wisconsin
- Patty Murray, Washington
- Tim Johnson, South Dakota
- Jack Reed, Rhode Island

Republicans

- Ranking Member Thad Cochran, Mississippi
- Mitch McConnell, Kentucky
- Richard Shelby, Alabama
- Kay Bailey Hutchinson, Texas
- Lamar Alexander, Tennessee
- Susan Collins, Maine
- Lisa Murkowski, Alaska
- Lindsey Graham, South Carolina
- Dan Coats, Indiana

Congress gives detailed instructions to the armed forces including such specifics as the number of personnel authorized for each service, and the number authorized to hold senior rank.

Title Ten of the U.S. Code deals with the Armed Forces. It is an omnibus. It has Subtitles for General Military Law, for the Army, Navy, and Marine Corps, the Air Force, and Reserve Components.

Then there are Parts within these Subtitles. For instance, the Army Subtitles includes "Parts" for Organization, Personnel, Training, Services, Supply, and Procurement. Finally each Part includes Chapters. Again using the Army as an example, Part II – Personnel has Chapters on Strength, Enlistments, Appointments in the Regular Army, Temporary Appointments, Active Duty Special Appointments, Assignments, Details, and Duties, Rank and Command, Miscellaneous Prohibitions and Penalties, Miscellaneous Rights and Benefits, Hospitalization, Decorations and Awards, Retirement for Length of Service, Retired Grade, Computation of Retired Pay, Civilian Employees, and Miscellaneous Investigation Requirements and Other Duties. It is easy to get bogged down in details when learning about the military.

The Constitution says very little about the federal courts and the federal courts have said very little about the military. In the 1970s military women won a few challenges to policies such as the Navy's prohibition on sea duty for women and the Marine Corps' separation for pregnancy, but civilian courts rarely accept jurisdiction in cases related to the military. Deference is the rule. Again, civilian courts are a minor player.

However, the military has its own courts and a justice system that is spelled out in the Uniform Code of Military Justice (UCMJ).[20] You can read all about it in Title 10, Subtitle A, Part II, Chapter 47.

Active duty personnel and reservists working full time are subject to the UCMJ even when off base and off duty. National Guard personnel are subject only when their unit has been federalized. Veterans under care in military hospitals and civilians accompanying the military during exercises are also covered.

In addition to offenses that are similar to those in civilian law such as rape and robbery, the UCMJ includes as violations such things as "contempt for officials," "malingering," "provoking speeches or gestures," and "conduct unbecoming an officer and a gentleman." Catch-all Article 134 encompasses "all disorders and neglects to the prejudice of good order and discipline in the armed forces, [and] all conduct of a nature to bring discredit upon the armed forces."

In general, there is Non-Judicial Punishment (NJP) administered by a commander for misconduct. In the Army and Air Force NJP is referred to as an Article 15, in the Navy as "Captain's Mast" or a "page 7," and in the Marines as an NJP or as "going to office hours." Possible punishments depend on rank and can include confinement to quarters, reduction in pay, forfeiture of pay, reduction in rank, or simply a reprimand. More serious infractions go to trial by Courts Martial.[21] A decision there can be appealed to a Court of Criminal Appeals and, at its discretion, to the United States Court of Appeals for the Armed Forces. A final appeal can be made to the U.S. Supreme Court.

Each of the four DOD services has a corps of lawyers called Judge Advocates or JAGs.

Rank

Rank matters. Ranks have names and insignia. Also, they are often referred to as numbered letters, e.g. E-1, E-2, . . . E-9 or O-1, O-2, . . . O-10. The letter stands for enlisted or officer; the number stands for the pay grade. Thus one can be referred to by letter and number or by title such as private, corporal, sergeant for the enlisted, or lieutenant, captain, major for officers. E-4s and above are also referred to as Noncommissioned Officers (NCOs). They often have important responsibilities – and more experience than the young officers who are their superiors and supervisors. Generals and admirals are referred to as flag officers; Navy Commanders and Captains, and Majors, Lieutenant Colonels, and Colonels in the other three services are known as field grade officers; lower-ranking officers are called company grade officers.

There is not a simple dichotomy between enlisted and officers. The Army, Navy, and Marines have an intermediate category referred to as Warrant Officers. Warrant Officers typically have a special and valuable skill which "warrants" a ranking above that of enlisted personnel even if they are not eligible to become officers.[22] In Figure 2.2 you see the ranks and insignia for the services. Note that the Navy "rates" rather than ranks its personnel and has insignia on the cuff as well as on the shoulder.[23]

Currently, there are no five star officers, and there is only one E-10 for each service. With limited exceptions each enlistee or officer begins at the bottom rank and proceeds step by step through the ranks. There is little horizontal entry. Also, in general, one moves up or one is out.

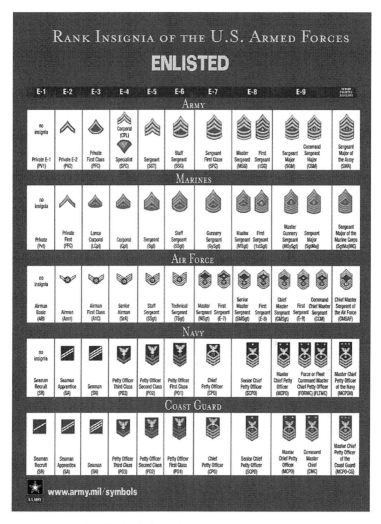

Figure 2.2 Rank and insignia charts. Source: www.defenselink.mil. (Continued overleaf.)

That is, if one is twice passed over for promotion, one does not simply stay at the rank achieved as one might do in a business or a civil service position; typically, one must leave the service.

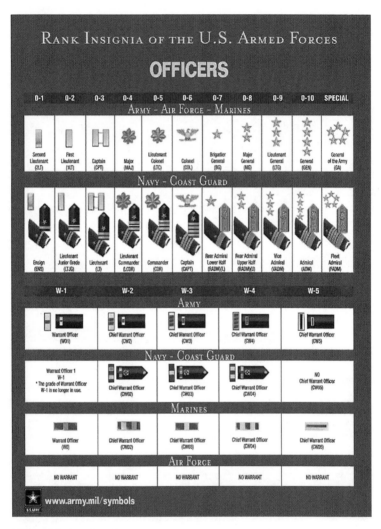

Figure 2.2 (continued)

The pace at which one is promoted depends upon the needs of the service. When the military is expanding, promotion can be rapid because senior leaders are needed; or, if senior leaders are leaving in large numbers, promotion may also be rapid. One becomes eligible for promotion at a prescribed time. That time involves total time in the military and time in the rank currently held. Individuals can be promoted early and they are not separated the first time they are passed over, although many choose to leave at that time rather than undergo a second evaluation.

Among enlisted personnel promotions are typically regular and rapid through E-4. Requirements are clear. Indeed, the Army has an 800-point system, which specifies a precise number of points for Duty Performance, Physical Readiness, Awards, Weapons Qualification, Military Education, Civilian Education, and Performance Board evaluation. Promotions become more competitive after E-4. Further, only a specified number of individuals can hold senior ranks. The result is that sometimes individuals are "selected" for promotion but they are not actually promoted until there is a vacancy. Also, all individuals at a specific rank do not compete against all others at the same rank. The military needs a specified number of individuals in particular specialties. Thus, one competes against others with the same specialty, and some specialties are more competitive than others. Thus, one's original choice of specialty can have a significant effect on one's career. It is possible to change specialties, but this varies by specialty and also by service.[24]

Uniforms

Although wearing a uniform emphasizes what is shared by those in the military, uniforms also distinguish each individual from every other individual. The first thing to notice is what service an individual belongs to and his or her rank or rate. In general, the Air Force wears blue, the Army has traditionally worn dark green with a light green shirt, the Navy dons midnight navy in cold weather, khaki in warm weather and on ship, and the Marines wear dark green with a khaki shirt.[25] However, men and women have different uniforms and officers and enlisted have different uniforms.[26] Further, there are dress and duty uniforms; there are winter and summer uniforms; there are physical fitness uniforms; there are battle dress and flight uniforms; there are desert camouflage and arctic uniforms; there are specialty uniforms;

and women's uniforms even include a maternity uniform. The military is notably a holdout for the wearing of hats.[27] Figures 2.3, 2.4, 2.5, and 2.6 show some frequently seen uniforms.

Uniforms can distinguish each individual from every other individual. In fact, most of the time one wears one's last name on the front of one's uniform. In addition, insignia tell one's rank and a variety of patches, pins, ribbons, badges, and tabs tell about an individual's training, for instance as a medic, one's tours, for instance to Iraq, and special assignments, for instance as a presidential honor guard or a recruiter. Further, Army, Marine, and Air Force units have an identifying patch.

Medals and ribbons are rightly a source of pride. Ribbons, which are 1¾ inches by ⅜ of an inch are composed of bands of bright colors. Each ribbon denotes something quite specific. They are worn on dress uniforms in an order of preference. Senior individuals may have so many ribbons that they are worn on a rack. If one is to work with military personnel, one should learn to "read" at least some of the most

Figure 2.3 General Peter Pace is wearing the Marine equivalent of a business uniform to testify to the Senate Armed Services Committee. Note his stars and rack of ribbons. DOD photo by Staff Sgt. D. Myles Cullen, U.S. Air Force. Source: www.army.mil.

Figure 2.4 These soldiers are nowhere near a desert, but camouflage uniforms are routinely worn for ordinary work days. Air Force Academy cadets even wear them to class four days a week. Photo credit: L. A. Shivley. Source: www.army.mil.

important ribbons. Two of the most well-known medals are the rarely awarded Medal of Honor (two have recently been awarded for service in Afghanistan and four for service in Iraq) and the Purple Heart, which is given to wounded personnel.

Command structures[28]

It is worth remembering that there is a "chain of command" that goes from the newest recruit to the President/Commander in Chief and vice versa. The Secretary of Defense is a key player. The President and the Secretary together are called the National Command Authority (NCA). There are three quite different command structures under the Secretary of Defense. One involves the Departments of the Army, Navy, and Air Force, each of which is led by a civilian secretary who reports to the Secretary of Defense. Their responsibility is to recruit, train, and equip. Thus, they prepare for, but have nothing to do with either planning or waging, war.

Figure 2.5 Those who fly wear their Air Force flight suits on a regular basis –
in the classroom, in the office, at a lecture. They do not have to be
in or near a plane. Source: www.army.mil.

Each of the military services also has a military chief appointed by
the President and confirmed by the Senate. They are the Chief of Staff
of the Air Force, the Chief of Staff of the Army, the Commandant of
the Marine Corps, and the Chief of Naval Operations. Each reports to
his respective civilian secretary and also serves on the Joint Chiefs of
Staff (JCS).

Figure 2.6 A change of command ceremony brings out Secretary of Defense Robert M. Gates, admirals in summer dress uniforms, and swords. DOD photo by Mass Communications Specialist 1st Class Chad J. McNeeley. Source: www.army.mil.

The Joint Chiefs of Staff consist of the four service chiefs plus a Chair and Vice Chair. In this role the Chiefs are expected to be "nonpartisan," that is to consider the military as a unified whole rather than as composed of separate services. The Chair of the JCS is the senior military advisor to the President, to the Secretary of Defense, and to the President's National Security Council. The Chair also has a responsibility to advise Congress. The staff is managed by a Director and is organized into eight sections, J-1 through 8. They are: Manpower and Personnel; Joint Staff Intelligence; Operations; Logistics; Strategic Plans and Policy; Command, Control, Communications and Computers (C4CS); Operational Plans and Joint Force Development; and Force Structure Resources and Assessment. It is important to remember that the JCS and its staff advise and plan. Importantly, they also do not have (war) command responsibilities although they plan for war.

The Goldwater–Nichols Act of 1986 provides for ten Unified Combatant Commands. These are the action-oriented, operational commands. There are ten Combatant Commanders, each of whom is a four star general or admiral who commands troops from two or more services. He (so far) reports to the Secretary of Defense, who reports to the President. These officers command the troops who are prepared to fight or who are actually fighting. There are geographic commands and functional commands. The six geographic commands are U.S. European Command, U.S. Pacific Command, U.S. Southern Command, U.S. African Command, which is new, U.S. Central Command, and U.S. Northern Command created after 9/11. Figure 2.7 indicates the area covered by each geographic command.

The four functional commands are U.S Transportation Command, U.S. Strategic Command, which merged with U.S. Space Command in 2002, U.S. Special Operations Command, and U.S. Joint Forces Command, which was closed down in late 2011.

In addition each service has a structure that includes a variety of commands. For example, the Army's dozen commands include Training and Doctrine, U.S. Army Europe, and Space and Missile. Its eleven direct reporting units include Medical, Intelligence and Security, and the U. S. Military Academy.

Further, the Army is organized into constituent units with a usual number of personnel led by individuals holding a usual rank. News accounts often refer to these units, particularly to companies, battalions, and brigades, and it is useful to know their approximate size and

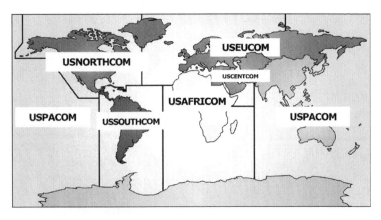

Figure 2.7 Map of geographic commands. Source: www.army.mil.

the rank of those who usually lead them. The Army is organized as in Table 2.1.

This is only an estimate because Army units vary in size depending on the specialty of the unit. The larger units, which are composed of a variety of specialties, vary depending on the specialties needed for a particular operation.[29] The Marines' organization is similar but not identical.

The Navy is composed of operating forces and a shore establishment whose mission is to support the operating forces. The Navy's operating forces have both administrative and operational chains of command. The administrative chain is responsible for training, logistics, budgetary support, and more. The operating forces include individual ships, submarines, aircraft, and the operational squadrons, strike groups, task forces, and numbered fleets under whose control the ships operate. The operational chain of command exercises control of operations. Particular units generally maintain the same administrative chain of command; however, the operational chain changes as the unit's mission and geographic location changes. The operating forces include numbered fleets which are organized by vessel.

The units are shown in Table 2.2.

Table 2.1 Organization of the Army

Name	Number	Leader
Squad	4–10	Staff Sergeant
Platoon	16–40, 3+ squads	Lieutenant
Company, Battery	100–200, 3+ platoons	Captain
Battalion	500–600, 3+ companies	Lieutenant Colonel
Brigade[a]	3,000–4,000, 3+ battalions	Colonel, Brigadier General
Division	10,000+, 3+ brigades	Major General
Corps	50,000+, 2+ divisions	Lieutenant General
Army	100,000+, 2–5 corps	General

a Brigades were once called regiments. Regiments no longer have a separate location in the table of organization, although some units have retained regimental names. The Army Air Cavalry call their companies "troops" and their battalions "squadrons." When you read about military deployments you are most likely to read about a battalion or brigade.

Table 2.2 Organization of Naval operating units

Name	Number	Leader
Task element	Single vessel	Captain or Commander
Flotilla	Small number of similar vessels	Rear Admiral (lower half)
Squadron, task unit	Three or four warships with support ships	Rear Admiral (lower half)
Strike Group	2+ task units	Rear Admiral (upper half)
Task force or battle fleet	2+ task groups	Vice Admiral
Fleet[a]	All vessels in a region	Admiral

a There are two principal fleets. The Atlantic Fleet consists of the 2nd fleet, which is being disbanded, and the 6th fleet, which provides ships to the European Command. The Pacific Fleet consists of the 3rd and 7th fleets. Both the Atlantic and Pacific Fleets provide ships for the 5th fleet under Central Command in the Persian Gulf and Arabian Sea. The 4th fleet supports Southern Command and the 10th fleet focuses on cyberwarfare.

The Strike Group typically consists of an aircraft carrier, four to six surface combatant ships, one or two submarines, and a supply vessel. A naval expeditionary force is typically organized for a very specific operation and then disbanded.

The Marine Corps is composed primarily of operating forces. The other units are the Marine Corps Reserve, the Support Establishment, and Headquarters. The basic operational unit is called a Marine Air–Ground Task Force (MAGTF), organized around a battalion, brigade, or division, which can include infantry, armor, amphibious vehicles, aircraft, artillery, and support units. Like the Navy's operational organization it is a temporary structure formed for a specific operation. An MAGTF varies in size, from a quickly deployable Marine Expeditionary Unit (MEU) composed of 2,200 marines and commanded by a colonel, to a Marine Expeditionary Force (MEF), which includes an infantry division, an air wing, and a logistics group and is commanded by a general. Marine Corps Divisions are headquartered at Camp Pendleton, at Camp Lejeune, and at Camp Courtney in Okinawa. A fourth division, which manages Reserve affairs, is located in New Orleans. Troops are

Table 2.3 Organization of the Air Force

Name	Personnel	Aircraft	Leader
Flight	20–100	4–6	Captain
Squadron	100–300	7–16	Lieutenant Colonel, Major
Group	300–1,000	17–48	Colonel
Wing	1,000–5,000	48–100	Colonel, Brigadier General
Numbered Force	By region	2+ Wings	Major General, Lieutenant General
Major Command	By function	Varies	General

organized like the Army into squads, platoons, companies, battalions, regiments (brigades) and divisions. Marine Aviation units are organized into sections, squadrons, groups and wings.

The Air Force has twelve commands including Air Combat, Air Education and Training, Air Force Global Strike, Air Force Materiel, Air Force Reserve, Air Force Space, Air Force Special Operations, Air Mobility, Air National Guard, Pacific Air Forces, U.S. Air Forces in Europe, and Air Force Cyber Space.

The Air Force organization (Table 2.3) includes the number of personnel, the number of aircraft, and the usual rank of the commander. Up to the Wing the planes are of a specific type, that is, are composed of fighters, bombers, tankers or whatever. Wings may be either specialized or composite; they are the primary operational unit.

Military specialties

Before the end of the draft and the use of large numbers of contractors there was a military ethic of self-sufficiency. This meant that the military was composed of many different specialties and that many members of the military served in noncombat roles. This remains true even though contractors now do many tasks the military once did itself. Specialties differ in the training required and in deployment and other requirements.

Army specialties fall into three basic categories: Combat, Combat Support, and Combat Service Support. Enlisted, officers, and warrant officers participate in each of these categories. Within these fields each enlisted individual has a Military Occupation Specialty Code (MOSC), which begins with two numbers. Those are the numbers that appear in the chart of enlisted career management fields shown below. Army officers have an Area of Concentration Code (AOC) which also begins with two numbers. These specialties are grouped into branches or functional areas as shown below. Upon commissioning an officer becomes a member of a branch with a numbered AOC. After several promotions s/he may move into a Functional Area (FA). Warrant officers have a similar Warrant Officer Military Occupational Specialty (WOMOS) code and specialties are grouped by branch. All soldiers wear insignia referring to their specialty. The fields for Army enlisted and officers are shown in Tables 2.4–2.7.[30]

Table 2.4 Army enlisted career management fields[a]

Combat Arms	Combat Support	Combat Service Support
11 – Infantry	21 – Engineer	27 – Paralegal
13 – Field Artillery	25 – Communications & Information Systems Operations	35 – Electronic Maintenance & Calibrations
14 – Air Defense Artillery		38 – Civil Affairs (RC)
		42 – Adjutant General
15 – Aviation	31 – Signal Operations	44 – Financial Management
18 – Special Forces	33 – Electronic Warfare/ Intercept System Maintenance	46 – Public Affairs
		55 – Ammunition
		56 – Religious Support
19 – Armor	37 – Psychological Ops	63 – Mechanical Maintenance
21 – Engineer	74 – Chemical	68 – Medical
	88 – Transportation	71 – Administration
	95 – Military Police	77 – Petroleum & Water
	96 – Military Intelligence	79 – Recruitment & Reenlistment
	98 – Signals Intelligence/ Electronic Warfare Ops	89 – Ammunition
		91 – Medical
		92 – Supply & Services
		94 – Electronic Maintenance & Calibrations
		97 – Bands

a Department of the Army Pamphlet 611–21, Part III provides a career progression figure for each CMF.

Table 2.5 Army officer branches

Combat Arms	Combat Support	Combat Service Support
11 – Infantry	25 – Signal Corps	38 – Civil Affairs
13 – Field Artillery	31 – Military Police	42 – Adjutant General Corps
14 – Air Defense	35 – Military	44 – Finance Corps
Artillery	Intelligence	67 – Medical Service Corps
15 – Aviation	74 – Chemical	88 – Transportation Corps
18 – Special Forces		89 – Ammunition
19 – Armor		91 – Ordnance
21 – Corps of		92 – Quartermaster Corps
Engineers		
		Special Branches:
		27 – Judge Advocate
		General's Corps
		56 – Chaplain
		60, 61, 62 – Medical Corps
		63 – Dental Corps
		64 – Veterinary Corps
		65 – Army Medical Specialist
		Corps
		66 – Army Nurse Corps

The Marine Corps divides its enlisted occupations into some forty Occupational Fields, each of which contains MOSs. Although the Marine Corps does include specialties such as Linguist, Legal Services, and Meteorology and Oceanography, the bulk of its personnel are in combat specialties. An individual's MOS changes as one advances in rank. Marine officer MOSs are nearly identical to those of enlisted MOSs but officers also can be recruiters and pilots. Again, individuals change MOS during the course of their career.

The Air Force Specialty Codes (AFSCs) are similar to the Army's MOSCs. Enlisted career groups include operations, maintenance/ logistics, support, medical/dental, legal/chaplain (an interesting conjunction), acquisition/finance, special investigation, and special duty. Each category has subfields which may have subdivisions. Also, the AFSC includes a number to identify the level of the individual's skill level from "helper" through "chief enlisted manager." Officer career groups are similar to those of enlisted and include a "qualified" identifier rather than a "skill level." Overall, the Air Force offers some 150

Table 2.6 Other Army areas of concentration by function

FA – AOC
24 – Systems Engineering
30 – Information Operations
34 – Strategic Intelligence
37 – Psychological Operations (add 0604)
38 – Civil Affairs
39 – Psychological Operations & Civil Affairs (del 0709)
40 – Space Operations
43 – Human Resource Management
45 – Comptroller
46 – Public Affairs
47 – U.S. Military Academy Stabilized Faculty
48 – Foreign Area Officer
49 – Operations Research/Systems Analysis (ORSA)
50 – Force Development
51 – Research, Development & Acquisition
52 – Nuclear Research & Operations
53 – Systems Automation Officer
57 – Simulations Operations
59 – Strategic Plans & Policy
70 – Health Services
71 – Laboratory Sciences
72 – Preventive Medicine Sciences
73 – Behavioral Sciences
90 – Logistics

Table 2.7 Army warrant officer branches

Combat Arms	Combat Support	Combat Service Support
13 – Field Artillery	21 – Corps of Engineers	27 – Judge Advocate General's Corps
14 – Air Defense Artillery	25 – Signal Corps	42 – Adjutant General's Corps
15 – Aviation	31 – Military Police	60 – Medical Corps
18 – Special Forces	35 – Military Intelligence	64 – Veterinary Corps
		67 – Medical Service Corps
		88 – Transportation Corps
		89 – Ammunition
		91 – Ordnance
		92 – Quartermaster Corps
		94 – Electronic Maintenance

different AFSCs to enlisted personnel. There are thirty career fields for officers with varying degrees of competitiveness and skill/training requirements.

The Navy, not unexpectedly, is different. It uses "ratings" for enlisted personnel and "designators" for officers.[31] One's "rating" is his or her specialty and a badge on the left sleeve designates that specialty.[32] The Navy's codes function much as the codes in the other services, showing first a general area of expertise such as Aviation, Construction, Administrative/Medical/Dental, or Engineering/Hull. There are many "advanced specialty" categories within each of these areas, which are designated by letters and with numbers indicating a subspecialty. For example, a Naval Corpsman who is in the Administrative Field has an HM rating. More specifically an HM-8407 is a Radiation Health Technician and an HM-8482 is a surgical technologist.

The Naval Officer Occupational Classification System (NOOCS) conveys a great deal of information about each officer. The code involves designator (specialty), grade, subspecialty, duties, and additional qualifications. Details are provided in a *two-volume* Naval Occupational Manual.[33] Naval officers are either line officers, whose insignia includes a star, or staff officers, who are professionals such as chaplains, physicians, and engineers and wear insignia denoting their profession. Limited Duty Officers and Commissioned Warrant Officers, who are mostly technicians, also wear insignia representing their expertise. Again, Navy enlisted do not have a rank. They have a rate, which indicates their pay grade, and a rating, which indicates their specialty. The two are combined in an insignia that indicates rate with chevrons and rating with a symbol. Figure 2.8 shows some rating (specialty) insignia.

Compensation and benefits

When the military became a volunteer force, compensation had to become competitive with civilian compensation. Figure 2.9 shows the basic monthly pay by rank and time in service. It is the same for all the services.

This is not the whole picture. Personnel who are not housed on base receive a housing allowance that varies by rank, time in service,

Figure 2.8 Navy specialty insignia. Source: www.defenselink.mil.

number of dependents, and zip code. They also receive a food (subsistence) allowance, dislocation allowance, family separation allowance, clothing allowance, and cost of living allowance in areas where the cost of living exceeds the country standard by at least 8 percent, as does Washington, DC, for example.

The military also provides pay for certain specialties such as diving and foreign language proficiency, for circumstances, such as a combat-related injury, and for submarine duty. A list of the most common categories for additional pay is shown below.

1.4% increase

MONTHLY BASIC PAY TABLE

EFFECTIVE 1 JANUARY 2011

YEARS OF SERVICE

COMMISSIONED OFFICERS

PAY GRADE	<2	2	3	4	6	8	10	12	14	16	18	20	22	24	26	28	30	32	34	36	38	40
O-10	0.00	0.00	0.00	0.00	0.00	0.00	0.00	0.00	0.00	0.00	0.00	14975.10	14975.10	14975.10	14975.10	14975.10	14975.10	14975.10	14975.10	14975.10	14975.10	14975.10
O-9	0.00	0.00	0.00	0.00	0.00	0.00	0.00	0.00	0.00	0.00	0.00	14975.10	14975.10	14975.10	14975.10	14975.10	14975.10	14975.10	14975.10	14975.10	14975.10	14975.10
O-8	9530.10	9842.70	10050.00	10107.90	10366.50	10798.20	10899.20	11308.80	11426.40	11779.80	12291.20	12762.30	12977.30	13077.30	13077.30	13077.30	13404.30	13404.30	13739.40	13739.40	13739.40	13739.40
O-7	7919.10	8237.70	8457.30	8592.60	8837.70	9079.80	9359.70	9630.70	9918.70	10776.20	10391.70	10391.70	10391.70	10831.70	11031.70	11031.70	11031.70	11031.70	11031.70	11031.70	11031.70	11031.70
O-6	4993.00	5512.20	5843.80	5965.80	6203.70	6346.20	6658.40	6883.20	7185.20	7640.70	7856.70	8070.30	8313.30	8313.30	8313.30	8313.30	8313.30	8313.30	8313.30	8313.30	8313.30	8313.30
O-5	4221.90	4887.30	5213.40	5286.00	5286.00	5588.70	5913.30	6317.40	6632.10	6951.10	7049.10	7145.10	7145.10	7145.10	7145.10	7145.10	7145.10	7145.10	7145.10	7145.10	7145.10	7145.10
O-4	3711.90	4298.10	4542.00	4651.80	4951.80	5188.80	5449.20	5894.70	6039.00	6317.40	6851.10	6976.50	7049.10	7049.10	7049.10	7049.10	7049.10	7049.10	7049.10	7049.10	7049.10	7049.10
O-3	3257.30	3652.80	3942.00	4294.30	4438.50	4659.30	4830.00	5078.70	5200.50	6039.00	6039.00	6039.00	6039.00	6039.00	6039.00	6039.00	6039.00	6039.00	6039.00	6039.00	6039.00	6039.00
O-2	2784.00	2897.40	3502.50	3502.50	3502.50	3502.50	3502.50	3502.50	3502.50	3502.50	3502.50	3502.50	3502.50	3502.50	3502.50	3502.50	3502.50	3502.50	3502.50	3502.50	3502.50	3502.50
O-1	2784.00	2897.40	3502.50	3502.50	3502.50	3502.50	3502.50	3502.50	3502.50	3502.50	3502.50	3502.50	3502.50	3502.50	3502.50	3502.50	3502.50	3502.50	3502.50	3502.50	3502.50	3502.50

COMMISSIONED OFFICERS WITH OVER 4 YEARS ACTIVE DUTY SERVICE AS AN ENLISTED MEMBER OR WARRANT OFFICER

PAY GRADE	<2	2	3	4	6	8	10	12	14	16	18	20	22	24	26	28	30	32	34	36	38	40
O-3E	0.00	0.00	0.00	4913.80	5188.80	5449.20	5617.80	5894.10	6128.10	6262.20	6444.90	6444.90	6444.90	6444.90	6444.90	6444.90	6444.90	6444.90	6444.90	6444.90	6444.90	6444.90
O-2E	0.00	0.00	0.00	4349.10	4438.50	4580.10	4818.60	5002.90	5140.20	5140.20	5140.20	5140.20	5140.20	5140.20	5140.20	5140.20	5140.20	5140.20	5140.20	5140.20	5140.20	5140.20
O-1E	0.00	0.00	0.00	3502.50	3602.50	3740.40	4020.30	4138.90	4256.20	4349.10	4349.10	4349.10	4349.10	4349.10	4349.10	4349.10	4349.10	4349.10	4349.10	4349.10	4349.10	4349.10

WARRANT OFFICERS

PAY GRADE	<2	2	3	4	6	8	10	12	14	16	18	20	22	24	26	28	30	32	34	36	38	40
W-5	0.00	0.00	0.00	0.00	0.00	0.00	0.00	0.00	0.00	0.00	0.00	6820.80	7167.00	7424.70	7710.00	7710.00	8095.80	8095.80	8500.50	8500.50	8925.90	8925.90
W-4	3836.10	4126.50	4245.00	4361.40	4562.10	4760.70	4961.40	5264.40	5529.60	5781.90	5988.30	6189.60	6485.40	6728.40	7005.60	7005.60	7145.70	7145.70	7145.70	7145.70	7145.70	7145.70
W-3	3502.80	3648.90	3798.60	3847.80	4004.70	4313.70	4635.00	4786.20	4961.10	5142.00	5466.00	5685.30	5816.40	5995.60	6144.90	6144.90	6144.90	6144.90	6144.90	6144.90	6144.90	6144.90
W-2	3099.90	3393.00	3483.30	3546.40	3746.40	4059.00	4213.50	4356.20	4552.50	4698.00	4830.00	4987.80	5091.60	5174.10	5174.10	5174.10	5174.10	5174.10	5174.10	5174.10	5174.10	5174.10
W-1	2721.00	3013.50	3092.40	3258.80	3456.00	3745.80	3881.40	4070.40	4256.70	4403.10	4538.10	4701.60	4701.60	4701.60	4701.60	4701.60	4701.60	4701.60	4701.60	4701.60	4701.60	4701.60

ENLISTED MEMBERS

PAY GRADE	<2	2	3	4	6	8	10	12	14	16	18	20	22	24	26	28	30	32	34	36	38	40
E-9	0.00	0.00	0.00	0.00	0.00	0.00	4638.70	4743.90	4872.00	5027.70	5184.60	5436.60	5649.30	5873.40	6215.70	6215.70	6526.20	6526.20	6852.90	6852.90	7196.80	7196.80
E-8	0.00	0.00	0.00	0.00	0.00	3794.10	3961.80	4065.60	4190.40	4325.10	4568.40	4691.70	4901.70	5017.80	5304.60	5304.60	5411.10	5411.10	5411.10	5411.10	5411.10	5411.10
E-7	2637.30	2878.50	2988.90	3135.00	3249.00	3444.60	3554.70	3750.90	3913.50	4024.50	4143.60	4189.20	4342.60	4425.60	4740.00	4740.00	4740.00	4740.00	4740.00	4740.00	4740.00	4740.00
E-6	2281.20	2510.10	2620.80	2728.50	2840.70	3093.60	3192.30	3382.80	3441.00	3483.60	3533.40	3533.40	3533.40	3533.40	3533.40	3533.40	3533.40	3533.40	3533.40	3533.40	3533.40	3533.40
E-5	2090.10	2230.20	2337.90	2448.30	2620.20	2800.50	2947.50	2965.50	2965.50	2965.50	2965.50	2965.50	2965.50	2965.50	2965.50	2965.50	2965.50	2965.50	2965.50	2965.50	2965.50	2965.50
E-4	1916.10	2014.20	2123.40	2230.80	2325.90	2325.90	2325.90	2325.90	2325.90	2325.90	2325.90	2325.90	2325.90	2325.90	2325.90	2325.90	2325.90	2325.90	2325.90	2325.90	2325.90	2325.90
E-3	1729.80	1838.70	1950.00	1950.00	1950.00	1950.00	1950.00	1950.00	1950.00	1950.00	1950.00	1950.00	1950.00	1950.00	1950.00	1950.00	1950.00	1950.00	1950.00	1950.00	1950.00	1950.00
E-2	1644.90	1644.90	1644.90	1644.90	1644.90	1644.90	1644.90	1644.90	1644.90	1644.90	1644.90	1644.90	1644.90	1644.90	1644.90	1644.90	1644.90	1644.90	1644.90	1644.90	1644.90	1644.90
E-1 >4 Mon	1467.60	1467.60	1467.60	1467.60	1467.60	1467.60	1467.60	1467.60	1467.60	1467.60	1467.60	1467.60	1467.60	1467.60	1467.60	1467.60	1467.60	1467.60	1467.60	1467.60	1467.60	1467.60
E-1 <4 Mon	1357.20	0.00	0.00	0.00	0.00	0.00	0.00	0.00	0.00	0.00	0.00	0.00	0.00	0.00	0.00	0.00	0.00	0.00	0.00	0.00	0.00	0.00

CFS 14975.10   M/S 7489.80

NOTE - BASIC PAY FOR O-7 TO O-10 IS LIMITED TO LEVEL II OF THE EXECUTIVE SCHEDULE ($14,975.10)
NOTE - BASIC PAY FOR O-6 AND BELOW IS LIMITED TO LEVEL V OF THE EXECUTIVE SCHEDULE ($12,141.60)

FY2011, 1.4% Pay Raise increase. Public Law No. 111-383 National Defense Auth Act,
signed into law on January 7, 2011
FY2011, increases cap on basic pay for general and flag officers (O7-O10)
Level II and Level V by 0.0%

Figure 2.9 Paytable. Source: www.defenselink.mil.

- Aviation Career Incentive Pay
- Hazardous Duty Incentive Pay
- Career Enlisted Flyer Incentive Pay
- Hostile Fire/Imminent Danger Pay
- Career Sea Pay
- Combat Related Injury and Rehab Pay
- Special Assigned Duty Pay
- Special Pay for Medical Officers (and Dentists and Veterinarians)
- Flight Pay, Submarine Pay, Special Warfare Pay
- Hardship Duty Pay

And there are more.

Finally the military does what it has to do. Thus, bonuses as large as necessary are used to enlist or retain the required specialties and numbers of personnel in uniform. During the second Iraq war some individuals received enlistment bonuses of $40,000 and some who reenlisted while in Iraq received bonuses which, in addition, were tax free.

There are other financial advantages such as Space A (free) travel (when available) including travel for families, veterans, and civilians working for DOD, and Space A (free or low-cost) stay at military bases. Military commissaries may save up to 30 percent for groceries, and gas purchased on a base is cheaper because no tax is paid. Further, states provide benefits to military members, their families, and veterans, and personnel are eligible for a variety of discounts in restaurants, at hotels, and at many stores including Home Depot, Dunkin Donuts, and Apple Computers.

An honorably discharged veteran's benefits include a pension after twenty years of service and education benefits after only three years of service under the GI Bill.[34] Vocational counseling and rehabilitation is available; so are home loan guarantees and a group life insurance plan.

Next we will consider the purpose of the military and its way of preparing to meet its challenges by considering strategy, the grand overview, and doctrine, the learned responses to anticipated challenges.

3   Strategy, doctrine, tactics, and skills[1]

Strategy

The United States has a National Security Strategy (NSS), which is prepared by the President's National Security Council. It includes economic and diplomatic components as well as a military component.[2] There is a substrategy, the National Military Strategy (NMS), which is prepared by the Joint Chiefs of Staff. That strategy is the product of lengthy discussion on the part of high-level military and civilians in different parts of the government.[3] Traditionally much of it is bland or stating the well-known. Rarely does either strategy become the subject of political debate, although President George W. Bush's first NSS included several positions which caused some angst. One was the assertion that pre-emption was a possibility, and the second was a stated willingness to go it alone when necessary. Pre-emption has never been renounced, nor has a commitment ever been made to always proceed with allies or with United Nations approval. Still, the Bush administration's assertions were seen by some as unusual and somewhat belligerent. As will be discussed below, Obama's NMS, which was not released until February 2011, is quite different in tone.

Obama's NSS rejects the concept of a Global War on Terror, stating that the enemy is Al Qaeda and its affiliates and that terror is a tactic not an adversary. The document establishes four principal interests: (1) security (including cyberspace and climate change), (2) prosperity (rooted in education, innovation and sustainability), (3) values (democracy, human rights, dignity), and (4) international order (including cooperation, alliances, and strengthening international standards and institutions). It commits to engaging with others and shifts discussions of economic policy from the G-8 to the G-20.

It is important to remember that strategy is the big picture. It involves a broad vision that takes into account many factors including geography, public opinion, and the reaction of allies – and of opponents. It also takes into account the future, and the consequences that are likely to follow from particular decisions.[4] Although something like a checklist may be devised to ensure breadth of analysis, thinking about the future is much more difficult. Further, the further into the future, five years or ten, the more difficult is prediction. Unintended consequences and unexpected events inevitably occur; they are the strategist's nemesis.

Strategy as taught at the Army War College late in the 1990s involved (1) defining the threat, (2) setting the goal, the end, and (3) selecting the best means to that end. That framework suggested that decisions about budget, weapons systems, and personnel would be driven by specific goals responding to specific threats to U.S. vital interests.

The 2011 NMS is quite different. First, instead of emphasizing threats and power, the theme is one of U.S. leadership, a leadership that always demonstrates U.S. core values. Second, instead of describing requirements to respond to specific threats, it refers to a full spectrum of "capabilities and attributes." Third, it stresses the importance of deepening relationships with allies and developing partnerships, including with "new and diverse groups of actors." Fourth, it emphasizes care for "our people and their families."[5]

Leadership, the NMS says, can involve support, for instance, of government agencies and/or civilian organizations. It can involve enabling and also the convening of other nations. It can also involve guaranteeing their security. Leadership is much more than command.

According to the NMS the big picture is one of more and more state and non-state actors able to have "consequential influence." This includes two "rising powers" in Asia and a number of "regionally consequential" powers in Asia and the Middle East.[6] It notes that demographics indicate a growing and urbanized global population, but with a decline in population in much of the developed world. It expresses concern that water scarcity may lead to conflict, and, in contrast, concern that rising ocean levels may threaten coastal cities. The U.S. economy, it states, will remain strong "though national debt poses a significant national security risk."[7] Also, reduced defense spending by NATO members may affect collective security. Of course, the importance of access to hydrocarbon resources (oil) hardly needs mention. The stated concern related to Iran's potential acquisition of nuclear weapons is not the possibility that it will target Israel or Europe, but that it will set off an arms race in the Middle East. Finally, a newly emphasized concern is "the global commons," sea, air, space, and cyberspace as well.

Four military objectives are specified. The first is to counter terrorist extremism. The chief effort is to defeat al Qaida (sic) and its affiliates in Afghanistan and Pakistan. It clearly acknowledges that extremism must finally be rejected by secure and prosperous populations living under a legitimate government. However, emphasis is also given to reliable and effective military-to-military relationships that persevere through "upheavals."[8] Also, acknowledging that terrorists are hard to target or deter directly, the NMS is clear that governments or entities "complicit" in an attack against the United States or its allies should be prepared for a response, which could include "the full spectrum" of military capabilities. Any force, though, will be "precise and principled," that is, collateral damage (civilian casualties) will be minimized. This is because it reduces the risk of turning people against us. Thus, strategic success is said to be aligned with both international law and our values.[9]

The second goal is to deter and defeat aggression. The U.S. nuclear arsenal is to be reduced but maintained, and a ballistic missile defense against limited attacks is to be advanced. WMD proliferation will be tackled in a variety of ways, but Combatant Commanders will conduct "prudent planning" to militarily eliminate sources of WMD. Conventional deterrence is said to rest on the ability to "rapidly and globally project power in all domains"; forces are to be "geographically distributed, operationally resilient and politically sustainable."[10] Of course, some countries may not approve of U.S. global reach and develop anti-access (no combat forces admitted) and area-denial (constraint of U.S. free action) strategies. U.S. counter strategies are numerous and include forcible entry. In particular, the United States commits itself to deterring any behavior that reduces access to the global commons or disrupts cyberspace connectedness.

The third goal, both immediate and long term, is to "strengthen international and regional security." This emphasizes U.S. forward presence and a capacity to rapidly shift forces from one region to another. Iran remains a principal concern and is a reason for a "long-term partnership with Iraq" including providing for Iraq's defense. Major changes are occurring in Asia; still the United States sees itself as maintaining a strong military presence in Northeast Asia (South Korea) for decades. There is also a desire to expand the range of military cooperation including multilateral exercises in Southeast and South Asia. China is, of course, the elephant in the room.[11] Although concerned about China's military modernization, the stated goal is a "positive, cooperative, and comprehensive relationship" including a deeper military-to-military relationship. Security is given a broad interpretation to include responding to trafficking, piracy, pandemics, and natural disasters. Again, the NMS weaves through all its exposition the themes of leadership and of cooperation with U.S. civilian agencies, with nation states, and with international organizations of all kinds.

The NMS's last goal involves U.S. forces. This includes developing more innovative and adaptable leaders capable of interacting with a wide variety of others, providing benefits and support for troops both while in service and after returning to civilian life, and assuring the public that the military will remain apolitical "at all costs." Acquisition costs are to be better managed but without sacrificing the U.S. margin of technical superiority or diminishing the U.S. industrial base. Some emphasis is given to intelligence, surveillance, and reconnaissance capabilities and, in particular, the need for more human intelligence.

As can be seen, strategy as set forth in the current NMS is not sufficiently specific to drive budget requests. It is the military's Quadrennial Review (QDR) that offers at least some specifics.

Although the QDR was published before the NMS, the documents are in harmony. The QDR begins by referring to "a complex and uncertain security landscape in which the pace of change continues to accelerate." It then lists a wide range of military and of non-military challenges including such things as changing technology, global information flow, rapid urbanization of the littoral, climate change, new strains of disease, demographic changes, competition for resources, and, oh yes, the proliferation of WMD. "Vital interests" are not cited. Instead, it is asserted that "America's interests . . . require armed forces with unmatched capabilities and a willingness . . . to employ them in defense of our interests and the common good."

Several important points emerge from that single sentence. First, the United States is to continue to have "unmatched capabilities." No nation will be allowed to catch up. Second, even though the United States is engaged in two wars, there is an emphasis on "will." This is tricky because it rests on the perception of others. A military or a weapon does not deter if others believe it will not be used. Further, if the United States makes too many commitments, enlists too many "partners and allies," the U.S. "will" can be tested in an infinite number of places, in an infinite number of ways and an infinite number of times. It makes the United States vulnerable to provocateurs that hit and run, that taunt, and correctly or mistakenly see the United States as the proverbial paper tiger.

The QDR's military goals are, essentially, those of the NMS. The first is to "prevail" by defeating Al Qaeda and eliminating its safe havens and by responsibly drawing down in Iraq. The second is to prevent and deter conflict, in concert with allies and partners, using a "whole-of-government" approach, which integrates defense with diplomacy and development.[12] In addition to conventional forces, military deterrence is said to require cyber, space, and nuclear capabilities, missile defense, and global basing. The third goal is to prepare for that "wide range of contingencies" including natural disasters, stabilizing fragile states, preventing mass atrocities, and supporting civil authorities at home.[13] Whereas the first goal is specific and public, goals two and three leave room for almost any initiative, anywhere, including intervening in the affairs of sovereign nations.[14]

Specific goals for the first commitment include a recently developed counterinsurgency strategy focused on protecting civilians, building the economy, and providing an adequate government with well-trained, local military and police forces.[15] No strategy is outlined for commitments two and three. This is because no goals are specified. Therefore, there are no clearly defined means, and, therefore, no guidelines as to what is needed in the way of budget, weapons, and personnel. Instead, the goal seems to be having every "capability" that might be needed.[16]

The QDR elaborates a need to "rebalance" the force in the direction of (1) protecting the homeland and (2) preparing for counterinsurgency, stability, and counterterrorism operations. To do the former the North American unified command was recently created and attention is being given to how the military should support civilian fire and police personnel.[17] Employing the Regular military domestically would be a major departure for the United States. Since the Civil War the principle of *posse comitatus* has prevented the domestic use of the military to enforce the law.[18] To better prepare for counterterrorism operations the QDR calls for more helicopters, more unmanned aircraft (drones), more special operations forces, and more doctrine and training in counterterrorism for Regular forces.[19]

The QDR also calls for building the capacity of "partner" states and calls for enhancing the linguistic and cultural abilities of U.S. forces.[20]And language and culture training is not just for officers. It is considered important that those with boots on the ground, those who daily interact with the nationals of a country, understand the culture so, at a minimum, as not to antagonize or insult. A second specific goal is to make partners more effective by training their aviation forces, and by expediting acquisition and transfer of "critical capabilities" to them.[21] U.S. support of this kind is wide-ranging and not always public. For example, few Americans would have known of U.S. involvement in Ethiopia until it assisted Ethiopia's 2006 invasion of Somalia.

"Anti-access environments" simply means nations that do not want the U.S. military to have access to their country or neighborhood, and, more particularly, those with the potential to keep us out should we want access. Thus, the QDR states that the U.S. needs to enhance its ability to defeat others' defensive systems. The QDR also assumes that the stationing of U.S. troops and the construction of U.S. bases abroad deters conflict. Therefore, it calls for enhancing our "forward posture."[22] Conversely, it calls for the expansion of a capacity for long-range strikes. In addition, it calls for the exploitation of subsurface capacities, for assuring access to space, and for securing cyberspace operations.[23]

The QDR does contain some very specific goals. These include the "rebirth" of the Aral Sea located in the former Soviet republics of Uzbekistan and Kazakhstan, cooperating with Mexico to detect tunnels into the United States, and the creation of a Civilian Expeditionary Workforce.[24]

One of the most important strategy issues involves nuclear weapons, and it has a specific and separate document called the Single Integrated Operational Plan (SIOP).[25] One goal is nonproliferation. The United States has particularly focused on preventing Iran's acquisition of such weapons. It has had to make peace with India's and Pakistan's programs and to accept the fact that North Korea has a limited arsenal. However, there is a second goal. It involves drastically cutting the number of weapons held by nuclear powers, particularly those in the arsenals of the United States and Russia. The New Strategic Arms Reduction Treaty (START, 2010) cuts deployed warheads to 1,550 each.[26] It also cuts delivery systems to 800 each. Achieving a reduction in nuclear weapons involves arguments about deterrence, missile defense, verification, and "nuclear umbrellas" such as the one the United States now offers to others, for instance, Taiwan. Engaging China and Russia as partners in maintaining a stable world order is also a strategy; the means to that strategy are still being developed.[27]

Doctrine

Once a strategy has been designed doctrine enters the picture. If current strategy seems nebulous, doctrine is the opposite. Doctrine mostly concerns operations, the level of analysis below strategy but above tactics. Doctrine is an authoritative statement concerning a set of principles and a set of terms that is carefully taught so that troops will have shared knowledge, and, therefore, predictable responses. It is intended to establish a common vocabulary and a common way of thinking. Doctrine does not change often, but, when it does, it can take effect in a short period of time. This is because it is written down and explicitly and precisely taught.[28]

Doctrine involves the implementation of strategy. It is found in the many manuals developed by each service. Many of these are public and accessible on line. It is worth investing some time in looking at some of the service's key manuals, for instance, FM1 The Army, NDP1 Naval Warfare, AFDD1 Air Force Basic Doctrine, and the Marine's MCDP Warfighting. Many of these manuals are lengthy and attend to minute details. For instance, even before the revision of the Army's FM 5 "The Operations Process" was complete, a document was issued specifying language changes. Some terms such as "criteria for success" and "staff estimate" were "rescinded." Some terms such as "command" and "planning" were "modified." Some terms such as "board" and "warfighting function" were introduced. Another official document directed that "civil considerations" replace "human terrain," "close combat" replace "red zone," and "operational environment" replace "battlespace."[29] Military language is intended to increase precision. Often it confounds.[30]

Tactics and skills

What much of the military does during peacetime is go to school to learn doctrine and/or tactics and skills; it then trains by practicing those skills and tactics and by applying doctrine. Tactics are the prescribed activities of small units within an operation; skills include technical skills such as map reading, but also interpersonal skills that facilitate leadership. Training and education are big enterprises. For example, the Army's Training and Doctrine Command (TRADOC) employs 27,000 soldiers and 11,000 civilians who operate thirty-two schools.[31]

TRADOC has two capstone doctrine manuals: FM 1 titled "The Army," last published in 2005, and FM 3–0 "Operations," published in 2008. Mastery is expected. FM 1 proceeds from a statement of the Army's creed, to a statement of its values, to ten functions, to vision, to full spectrum operations (meaning operations that include offense, defense, and stability or civil support operations), to current, to future force, and, finally, Army campaign objectives. FM 3 "Operations" offers planners and executors of action something like a universal check list. Again, each service has manuals establishing doctrine. They represent crucial, shared knowledge rooted in experience.

The single manual best known to civilians is probably the U.S. Army/Marine Corps Counterinsurgency Field Manual, Army Manual 3–24/Marine Manual 3–033.5. Often credited to General David

Petraeus, the manual is, as is typical, the result of collaboration.[32] The manual was featured in *Newsweek* and published by the University of Chicago Press. The introduction to the Press volume was written by an expert on human rights policy who wrote that "Those who fail to see the manual as radical probably don't understand it."[33]

It is radical because the primary goal is defined as protection of civilians rather than attacking the enemy. Also, it deemphasizes force protection (of U.S. troops) in order to reduce civilian deaths, and it calls on U.S. civilians to accept more responsibility while at the same time preparing troops to accept political/diplomatic and economic roles "as necessary." While stressing adaptability, and local and small unit decision making, the manual, nevertheless, offers more than 400 pages of advice. Items include:

* Engage the Women; Be Cautious around Children
* Lose Moral Legitimacy, Lose the War
* Map the Social Structure
* Some of the Best Weapons for Counterinsurgents Do Not Shoot
* Remember the Global Audience.

The Army alone has hundreds of manuals. You can see a list of its doctrine and training manuals at http://armypubs.army.mil/doctrine/Active_FM.html. In many cases you can access a particular manual by googling it. A password is required to access it from the above site. Some titles are "Human Intelligence Collector Operations," "Counterintelligence," "Patriot [missile] Tactics, Techniques, and Procedures," "Survival," "Potential Military Chemical/Biological Agents and Compounds," "The Infantry Rifle Company," "Military Police Operations," "Field Hygiene and Sanitation," and "Jungle Operations."

The Air Force lists its publications at www.e-publishing.af.mil/. Its "product index" lists publications first by source and then by topic. The doctrine series, AFDD, are listed under "Departmental" publications. The department also issues thirty-five to forty series of Air Force Instructions (AFIs). The series, with titles such as "Logistics," "History," and "Safety," each include a number of AFIs. Headquarters Air Force has another set of some forty publications including

"Reduction in Force Benefit Guide," "Manual for Courts Martial United States," and "Legislative Liaison." The Air National Guard is a third source of publications.[34]

The Navy has six capstone statements of doctrine. The titles include "Naval Warfare," "Naval Intelligence," "Naval Operations," "Naval Logistics," and "Naval Command and Control." "Naval Warfare" is the fundamental text and is divided into four sections: "Who We Are: The Nature of Naval Services"; "What We Do: Employment of Naval Forces"; "How We Fight: Naval Warfare"; and "Where We Are Headed: Into the 21st Century." Again, these are available on the internet and the first, in particular, is worth a look. The Navy also issues "Instructions." These can be found at http://doni.daps.dla.mil/allin-structions.aspx. These are neatly arranged in thirteen folders including "Military Personnel Support," "Facilities and Land Management Ashore," and "Ordnance Material Management and Support." Lest you think things are simpler in the Navy, there is a more than sixty-page Instruction on issuing Instructions.

The Marine Corps is responsible for its own doctrine and other publications. Its ten doctrinal publications include four capstone booklets: "Warfighting," "Strategy," "Marine Corps Operations," and "Tactics." These and six "Keystone" publications are available on the web at www.doctrine.quantico.usmc.mil/aspweb/mcdp.asp.

Like the other services, the Marines have a nearly infinite variety of manuals, booklets, and other official publications telling the troops such things as how to survive in the wilderness and how to train as a sniper.

In recent years the Joint Forces Command has issued its own documents laying out doctrine and tactics when two or more services are conducting operations together.[35] Further, nonmilitary publishers may issue documents with official content as the University of Chicago Press did with the *Counterinsurgency Field Manual*, and they may also issue handbooks, often written by retired military personnel, which may be more usable than official documents. One example would be *Handbook for Marine NCO's* published by the Naval Institute Press,[36] now in its fifth or sixth edition.

The detailed and comprehensive nature of the hundreds of military publications may boggle the civilian mind,[37] but there are two good reasons for their existence and nature. The first is that shared knowledge makes the frequent rotation of personnel possible. It makes it possible for units that have never trained together to coordinate their actions quickly and effectively.

A second important reason for so much detail is that military personnel, even quite junior troops, are given heavy responsibilities for each other, for equipment, for information, for making decisions, and more. This is possible because thorough instruction and training means young troops know just what they are to do and can respond quickly and appropriately in a variety of situations.[38]

Because doctrine and responsibilities change as one is promoted, learning, formal, as well as on-the-job learning, and training are constant. Again, learning is what troops do for much of their day; indeed, much of their career.

4 The military in action

Recruitment, training, and education

After the draft ended in 1973, recruitment of new members of the military required more time and energy than expected. One remedy was to gradually but significantly increase the percentage of women in the military from less than 2 to today's 14 percent. If war is being waged, recruitment becomes more difficult. Another solution was to offer enlistment and reenlistment bonuses, which in some cases were as large as $40,000.[1]

The military does what it has to do: when necessary, it not only offers bonuses but lowers standards to meet its goals. However, it prefers to enlist physically and mentally fit high school graduates of good character and with a good credit rating. Recruiting is a full-time assignment and each recruiter is assigned a monthly goal.[2] In difficult times that goal may be as low as one or two recruits a month.[3] The goal is also likely to stipulate the expected number of men in comparison with women and the number for whom waivers may be given, for example, for someone without a high school degree or with some kind of court record.

The recruitment process can take several months and may involve a number of interviews, including interviews with the young person's parents.[4] The recruit must take a physical and the Armed Services Vocational Aptitude Battery (ASVAB) test. The different services may require different ASVAB minimum scores, as may different specialties. The recruiter's task, though, is to steer the recruit to specialties where the military has a shortage even if the potential recruit has a clear, different preference. Typically, a commitment of six years is required: four on active duty and two in the Reserves; however, specialties that require extensive training may require a longer commitment.

The services use ad campaigns and video games and have offices to welcome potential recruits. However, recruiters spend a lot of their time at high schools, in malls, and in other places where they might have the chance to talk to young men (especially). Recruiters know which areas (rural and urban rather than suburban, south and central rather than the coasts) are most likely to yield recruits.

Once a contract is signed, a recruit reports for basic training. The Navy's boot camp, or basic, is conducted at Great Lakes Naval Training Center north of Chicago. The Army's Basic Combat Training (BCT) is conducted in four locations, Fort Jackson, North Carolina, Fort Benning, Georgia, Fort Sill, Oklahoma, and Fort Knox, Kentucky. The Marines train for twelve weeks at Paris Island, South Carolina. The Air Force's basic occurs at Lackland Air Force Base in San Antonio, Texas.

Basic's indignities and stress, physical and mental, are designed to convert the individual from a civilian to a "STRACT" member of the military. New recruits are "broken down" and then "built up," and, at least at first, are intended to feel they cannot succeed. However, the trainers' goal is actually to get most of them through basic and on to a school or their first assignment. Importantly, part of the program is to build teamwork. Recruits soon learn that getting through, whether it is the obstacle course or preparing for inspection, requires cooperation, not competition.[5] The services emphasize different things. For instance, the Navy requires recruits to pass a swimming test, the Air Force gives emphasis to security and defensive fighting, the Army introduces hand-to-hand combat training in week two for both men and women, and the Marines train women and men separately. In every instance the physical standards which must be met are different for men and women. This is because the tests are not designed to meet physical requirements related to a recruit's future duties; the tests are designed to ensure fitness and to require significant effort.[6] The differences in men's and women's physiology account for the fact that different standards are needed to require similar effort and to achieve the same level of fitness for women and men.[7]

Civilians are likely to have some familiarity with basic training through movies, memoirs and fiction. That, however, is just the beginning. Members of the military train and go to school throughout their careers. Even new generals and admirals must attend a six-week Capstone course.[8] Members of the various services attend the same small Capstone course, which emphasizes strategy and joint operations and involves mostly briefings and field trips rather than reading and writing.

There are some schools and courses which prepare individuals for new responsibilities as they are promoted; others teach particular skills. Some involve residence; others can be taken on line. Further, the military encourages members to work toward degrees in civilian institutions while on active duty.[9]

Professional Military Education (PME) for officers has three levels. At the primary level the officer typically focuses on the career field or branch in which the individual will be serving, for example, military police, infantry. The intermediate level for lieutenant commanders and majors involves a Command and Staff College, which expands the student's horizons beyond his/her specialty, or a Joint Warfighting School, which expands the student's view beyond his/her service. Commanders and captains and lieutenant colonels and colonels attend the senior level schools, in particular, the War Colleges and the National Defense University. Some attend schools in other countries such as Argentina or Japan, and students from other militaries attend U.S. intermediate and senior level schools. In fact, as many as 9000 foreign students a year may attend a U.S. military school or take a course offered by the U.S. military in the United States.

The highly competitive U.S. Air Force, Military (West Point), and Naval Academies offer civilian accredited bachelor's degrees and a commission as an officer upon graduation. Less familiar are a variety of almost thirty other DOD schools, which offer accredited associate, master's, and PhD degrees. A Uniformed Services University even offers the MD and graduate work in Nursing.

Planning and research

Planning and research are vital activities. Planning is the responsibility of military officers and DOD civilians although contributions are sometimes made by civilian contractors and by researchers located in universities and think tanks. For instance, a Mass Atrocity Response

Operations (MARO) Handbook was recently developed at Harvard's Kennedy School in conjunction with the U.S. Army's Peacekeeping and Stability Operations Institute and the Humanity United Foundation, a nongovernmental organization (NGO).

In any large organization, planning is essential. For example, military weapons may require years to develop, test, and produce. As new weapons and equipment are put in place, old ones must be mothballed, sold, or destroyed. Resources may be required for a decade or longer, but appropriations are constitutionally limited to two years. This means even a well-designed plan can be disrupted by a later change in perceived threat, by Congressional decision, or hitches in development and cost overruns.[10] In contrast, planning for force strength is for the short term and routine, but it is not uncomplicated since it involves setting and then achieving a specific number of new recruits, a specific number of personnel for each service, a specific number for different specialties, and a specific number at different ranks. "Force management" also involves providing incentives to retain those who are needed, and "riffing" (involuntary discharging) those who are surplus, even some who have excellent evaluations.

The regular rotation of forces that must be supported/supplied throughout the globe requires skilled logistical plans.[11] Plans must also exist for emergencies. Just as it is hard to fathom the number and detail of DOD doctrinal, educational, and training documents, it is hard to convey how numerous and detailed military plans are. The Joint Chiefs of Staff has a responsibility for strategic planning and insuring troop readiness. It gives advice, but it is the chiefs of the unified combatant commands who prepare the operational plans and they do not report to the civilian secretaries or to their military chiefs or even to the joint chiefs. They report to the Secretary of Defense and he (so far) reports to the President. Theirs are the war plans. They are the ones who are tasked to have a plan for every contingency. These plans are mostly secret. However, knowing the military's penchant for completeness and worst case scenarios one can be sure they are numerous and that they deal with the defense of the United States and with potential humanitarian and peacekeeping missions as well as with go-to-war plans (OPPLANS). Some of the latter will be thoroughly developed including logistics and target lists. There is certainly a plan for Iran and possibly one for China. Other plans will be less developed concept plans (CONPLANS). Each geographic commander will at least have some CONPLANS. There may also be several plans for one region, for example the Korean peninsula. All plans require well-developed intelligence about the military, government, and even culture of a potential adversary; they can take months to prepare. Perhaps the most important plans are plans related to cyber and space warfare.

One great advantage of the U.S. military is its advanced technology.[12] Although some of that technology is wholly developed by civilian enterprises, the Office of Management and the Budget (OMB) estimates that in 2010 over $83 billion of the federal budget will be spent on research and development promoting national defense.[13] The services have their own research and development budgets, but after the USSR launched Sputnik in 1957 the United States created the Defense Advanced Research Program Agency (DARPA). Its mission is to ensure U.S. technology is always the most advanced. Its goal is not just to avoid surprise, but to create it. Its projects are intended to be "high risk–high payoff." DARPA has no labs but contracts projects to government and civilian labs and researchers. Perhaps its most revolutionary work involved the creation of personal computing, the internet, and the global positioning system. The public knows about its Grand Challenge Robot Race and its Hundred Year Starship plan to send humans to colonize, that is, not come back from, space. However, some DARPA research is classified. Its range includes biology, mathematics, social science, and neuroscience as well as the more obvious fields of engineering, physics, and computing. One of its most recent projects is a study to determine whether scanning email can detect whether or not a military member might be prone to either suicide or homicide.[14]

Intelligence

Collecting, analyzing, and using intelligence are crucial military functions. Intelligence absorbs a significant share of DOD resources although the public is rarely aware of the names of the different intelligence agencies, much less of the extent or the content of the work they do.

In 2004 Congress created the position of Director of National Intelligence to coordinate the work of the sixteen intelligence organizations within the federal government. Half of these are civilian agencies, some of whose names are familiar: the Central Intelligence Agency (CIA), the Federal Bureau of Investigation (FBI), and the Drug Enforcement Agency (DEA).[15] Eight are DOD agencies. Each of the four services has its own intelligence unit. In addition there is the Defense Intelligence Agency (DIA), which coordinates service intelligence agencies and works closely with the State Department and its embassies,[16] the National Geospatial Intelligence Agency (NGA) with extraordinary map expertise, which until 2004 was called the National Imagery and Mapping Agency, the National Reconnaissance Office (NRO), which focuses on what one can learn using satellites, including what is happening in space, and the National Security Agency (NSA), which focuses on communications. The NSA intercepts foreign communications whether sent by phone, pager, radio, radar, microwave, the internet, satellite, undersea cable, or other means. It not only intercepts, but has the task of decoding encrypted messages. A third and crucial mission is to protect U.S. cyber networks. Not long ago the NSA was involved in a controversy over warrantless surveillance of U.S. citizens in its enthusiastic, vacuuming approach to the collection of data.

Intelligence units collect information and analyze it. They then pass it on to those who need it and/or store it for future use. Usually, analysts have to be citizens without relatives living in a country where they might be subjected to pressure. They must also meet a number of other criteria for a security clearance; those criteria vary by level of clearance.[17] Levels include confidential, secret, and top secret. A particular level does not grant broad, automatic access. One also "needs to know." There are likely other levels and restrictions as well.

Intelligence employees mostly have a particular skill and a particular assignment; few are positioned to see the overall picture. Although officers are more likely to see the big picture, even they usually specialize in a specific field such as imagery, counterintelligence, signals, or human intelligence. Many of those working in intelligence are enlisted personnel or civilian employees or even contractors. Again, their work is mostly specialized and narrowly focused.

Most analysts, both civilian and military, have office jobs and much of the information they collect is public or "open source." However, some is not. Much of the latter is acquired at a distance and through the use of technology. Some of it, though, does involve human intelligence (HUMINT). This includes spies but also information acquired from individuals who may or may not be "witting," that is, may or may not know that they are contributing information. Information can come from many different individuals including foreign diplomats, prisoners of war (POWs), refugees, travelers, even employees of NGOs and businesses. Under-cover agents are not as numerous as fiction would have it, but they can be very valuable.[18] This is especially true in countries or areas where the United States has limited access.

DOD intelligence agencies may also have covert operational units. The American public is unlikely to know about their operations even if the foreign country where the operations take place is well aware of what is going on. The foreign country may be pleased to have U.S. personnel there, or it may be displeased. Even if it is displeased, it may not reveal what it knows because doing so would reveal its vulnerability.

As is typical of the military, intelligence has three levels: strategic, operational, and tactical. At the strategic level, analysis of the economic, political, and social structure of an enemy or threat is important. At the operational level, the commander wants to know all he can about the environment in which he will be operating. This would include not only information about enemy forces, but information about in-place civilians, the weather, and the topography. At the tactical level the focus is more on the enemy, his location, his weapons, his supply lines.

Three continuing problems plague the intelligence community. One is the issue of sharing information. Sharing may need to be done within and between agencies. Then there are issues about sharing with civilian officials, local, state, and tribal, and further issues about sharing with allies and partners. A second problem involves how to assemble the most important information from the huge volume of information collected. Much of the sorting is done by computer; humans could not begin to tackle the mountain of data collected.[19] A third concern involves the preservation of U.S. citizens' rights and privacy. Congress and some nonprofits such as the American Civil Liberties Union (ACLU) tend to serve as watchdogs. On occasion the executive branch has taken positions based on "necessity" that Congress has not supported.[20]

There is an effort to keep intelligence budgets and activities below the radar, but one estimate is that overall spending on intelligence comes to $80 billion a year.[21] One educated guess assigns 80 percent of that budget, $67 billion, to DOD agencies. Service intelligence agencies may receive a total of $27 billion and NSA and NRO are thought to receive $15 billion each. The number of employees is difficult to estimate but a photo shows that at NSA's main location there are no fewer than 18,000 parking places.[22] Sometimes additional information about the intelligence community can be obtained through Freedom of Information Act requests. Sometimes there is an inadvertent or intentional leak of information.

Diplomacy

Diplomacy? Don't militaries threaten and use force? Isn't diplomacy the job of the State Department? Well, yes, but there are many times and places that the military's strategy is persuasion and/or negotiation. Indeed, the military's intensive training in leadership largely focuses on persuading others to enthusiastically undertake whatever assignment they are given. Further, there are tasks that might appropriately be civilian tasks, but, realistically, only the military can carry out.

Think of a natural disaster halfway around the world: a volcano erupting in Indonesia, or a flood in Pakistan. The U.S. military's logistical capacity makes it possible to bring resources quickly to the stricken area. If sustained and fairly distributed, such aid makes friends for the United States.

In Afghanistan beginning in 2003 and in Iraq beginning in 2005 the United States and its allies developed Provincial Reconstruction Teams (PRTs) composed of both civilians and military personnel. In Afghanistan a PRT of perhaps 60–100 is typically commanded by a lieutenant colonel with military members and also civilians from USAID, the Department of Justice, the Department of Agriculture, and other units. In Iraq a PRT is more likely to be led by a State Department official. PRT tasks include enhancing local security, support for government, and reconstruction, for example of schools, roads and clinics.

Again, the intent is to contribute but also to influence, to win new friends. Independent humanitarian and development NGOs such as Doctors Without Borders and the International Committee of the Red Cross are likely to be operating in the same locations. Indeed, some independent NGOs believe that the use of PRTs in relief and reconstruction casts doubt on NGO neutrality and endangers their workers.

The U.S. military puts resources and energy into enabling its own forces, the Army, Air Force, Navy, and Marines, to work cooperatively. When the U.S. military participates in a coalition – for instance, the Multi National Force Iraq (MNF-I), which was originally composed of thirty-eight countries – the task becomes infinitely more complex; any coalition commander must exercise significant diplomatic skills. The fact that many of the Iraq coalition members had their own rules of engagement, or in Japan's case non-engagement, made anything approaching a unified command a challenge.[23]

A variety of treaties and alliances have military components. These include the North Atlantic Treaty Organization (NATO) and the Organization for Security and Co-operation in Europe (OSCE). In addition the United States has a variety of mutual assistance and security treaties. Even if a civilian President and the Senate authorize such agreements, senior military officers participate in the negotiations, have implementing duties, and may work closely with their military counterparts. Indeed, there are a variety of regular military-to-military contacts and exercises, and the DOD budget contains substantial amounts for the education of foreign officers and for equipment and technical assistance to foreign militaries. These activities are referred to as "engagement" and "building partner capacity." These activities are not restricted to allies; in fact, the U.S. military has been urging more direct contact with the Chinese military.

The United States has bases throughout the globe. In addition to their military duties, base commanders have a responsibility to develop good relations with local officials and dignitaries. They must also prevent friction between troops and the local population. Regulations for off-base conduct vary by location. What would be acceptable behavior is quite different in Germany, Korea, and Saudi Arabia. Wherever U.S. troops are stationed, Status of Forces Agreements (SOFAs) are negotiated. These cover a range of issues from taxation to postal service.

Controversies, though, are most often related to civil or criminal offenses by an American and can create an outcry.[24] Generally, the United States retains jurisdiction over offenses committed while on duty, but may yield jurisdiction for offenses committed off duty. A difficulty involves the fact that other countries' legal systems can be quite different from that of the United States. For example, Japan, where some 35,000 U.S. troops are stationed, had no jury trials until 2009.

Diplomacy has to be practiced at home, too. Base commanders have concerns for local outreach. Officers and senior enlisted especially are encouraged to participate in civic events, to coach American Youth Soccer or to lead a Scout troop. Civilians are invited to the base for special events, troops participate in Veteran's Day Parades – a "Good Neighbor" policy is a priority. A "Good Behavior" policy for off-duty personnel is also a priority.

In some communities a military base is a major contributor to the local economy and closing a base which is no longer needed becomes politically difficult. For this reason an independent, bipartisan Base Realignment and Closure (BRAC) commission was created in 1988. The fifth round of BRAC closures and realignments was initiated in 2005 and is to be completed by 2011. Although the plan calls for 100 actions in 800 locations and involves returning 15,000 troops to the United States and relocating 123,000 personnel, it does not, in fact, include a lot of closing. There is more "realignment."

There are two other important "diplomatic" activities. One involves public affairs activities vis à vis the military's own personnel, the media, and the American public. The second involves the military's relationship with Congress.

DOD Public Affairs provides enormous amounts of information through old-fashioned channels such as press briefings and conferences, news releases, public addresses, and *Stars and Stripes*; it also offers blogs, Facebook entries, podcasts, and widgets. It even has an Armed Forces Press Service (AFPS). On the one hand, military public affairs offerings are very like those of other government organizations or those of large corporations. On the other hand, they are subject to amazingly detailed regulations and guidance. For instance, a February 2003 guidance on embedded media specifically noted that "lipstick on combat sorties is approved and encouraged to the greatest extent possible."

Public Affairs is a military specialty; many with the specialty have attended the Defense Information School at Fort Meade, Maryland.

The practice of formally "embedding" the press in military units began in 2003 in Iraq. Many in the U.S. military believed that the U.S. media had harmed its efforts in Vietnam, which was the first war to bring military action to living room TV sets. During the first Iraq War and the invasion of Afghanistan the media had very limited access to U.S. troops in action. Therefore, the experiment in embedding was put into place. It involves commitments by the press to maintain necessary secrecy and to train for life on the front lines. In exchange they are provided transportation and security (at least the same security as enjoyed by the troops). The military seems to be comfortable with embedding, as are some journalists. Other journalists are wary.

Liaison officers connect the military to "significant others." A particularly important liaison is that between DOD and the U.S. Congress. The services have a Congressional Fellowship Program and well-stocked Offices of Legislative Affairs (Navy and Marines) and Offices of Legislative Liaison (Army and Air Force). The Army's Chief Legislative Liaison "ensures the overall integration of the Army's affairs with Congress, develops comprehensive Congressional engagement strategies for Army senior leaders, and disseminates critical information on all major Congressional activities" (http://ocll. hqda.pentagon.mil, accessed October 19, 2011). The Marine's Office "facilitates a shared understanding between the USMC and Congress in order to ensure support for the Commandant's legislative priorities and requirements" (www.marines.mil/unit/hqmc/cmclegalasst/Pages/ home.aspx, accessed October 19, 2011). The point is: the services do not just respond to the Congress. Their educative function sometimes gives the appearance of lobbying.

Training and advising around the globe

The *Military Times* publishes an annual guide to U.S. military installations titled "Installations Worldwide." The 2011 guide lists more than 400 bases, posts, and stations.

Those in the United States are concentrated in California and the south. According to the guide the only states with no installation directly under DOD are Oregon, Minnesota, Iowa, Vermont, and New Hampshire.[25] The guide provides phone numbers, details about units stationed there, population at the base and in the area. It even includes median price of housing in the area and climate information.

What civilians may not grasp is how many installations the United States has outside the country.

The Army has bases in Belgium, Germany (eleven of them), Italy, Japan, Kosovo, South Korea (five of them). The Navy has personnel on patrol on and under the sea at all times. In addition it has personnel at installations in the Bahamas, Bahrain, Cuba, Diego Garcia, Greece, Guam, Italy, Japan, Singapore, Spain, and South Korea. The reach of the Air Force extends to Germany, Greenland, Guam, Italy, Japan (three bases), Portugal, South Korea, Spain, Turkey, and the United Kingdom (five locations). The Marines mostly get transported to where the action is. They have only three foreign installations, all of them in Japan. These semipermanent installations give the United States a large global footprint.[26]

Of course, base locations do not tell the whole story. First, as 2011 began there were 100,000 U.S. troops in Afghanistan and 50,000 more in Iraq. Nearby Gulf states such as Kuwait, Qatar, and the United Arab Emirates have accepted U.S. missiles, Bahrain hosts the Fifth Fleet, and Kyrgyzstan and Uzbekistan, formerly part of the Soviet Union, provide access to Afghanistan for U.S. troops. Second, the Navy has thousands of personnel at sea. Third, there are troops on classified missions. These may be operating in Pakistan, Iran, Somalia, and Colombia among other places.[27] Fourth, there are troops in numerous countries who are "training" and/or "advising" other countries' militaries. These missions may be relatively small and often troops rotate in and out for rather short periods. There are a wide variety of missions. In Australia U.S. troops track satellites; in Israel they man radar stations. Some missions involve training for U.S. troops in different climates and geography. Some permit the two militaries to learn about each other's practices and capabilities. Others involve training locals on new equipment provided by the United States. U.S. troops may even accompany other nations' troops on patrol. It is these small missions which give rise to the large numbers for troops abroad cited by scholars such as Chalmers Johnson, who described the U.S. footprint as including 737 bases in 130 countries.[28] One further note: one reason for the many bases is to provide "forward presence".[29] The Navy, too, provides a great deal of presence even though its "footprint" is limited.

Uses of the military: humanitarian aid, intervention, surveillance and more

It has already been noted that because of its logistical capacity the military can play an important role in an emergency whether here or abroad. In this country that role is usually played by the National Guard. However, since 9/11 and the creation of the Department of Homeland Security and of the Northern Command, more attention has been paid to planning and coordinating the work of the Regular military with civilian agencies.

The U.S. military intervenes in a variety of situations without going to war. Interventions have a variety of names. One encompassing phrase is Military Operations Other than War (MOOTW); another is Low Intensity Conflict (LIC); another is Fourth Generation Warfare, which focuses on conflict with a nonstate enemy. Then there is asymmetric and irregular warfare. The point is: interventions became more frequent and more varied following the collapse of the Soviet Union. After 9/11 they may have increased even more.

Peace Operations are one kind of intervention. These include peacekeeping, peacemaking, peace building, and peace enforcement. Classical peacekeeping had three principles: (1) being invited by all parties to a conflict, (2) absolute neutrality, and (3) no use of force except in self-defense. Neither the United States nor the USSR participated much in classical peacekeeping since it was hard to think of either of them as genuinely neutral.[30] After the USSR collapsed a whole variety of other peace operations were developed with various degrees of neutrality and rules about the use of force called rules of engagement (ROE). The 1995 massacre at Srebrenica, which occurred while soldiers practicing the classical rules stood by, was one impulse toward United Nations Security Resolution 1674 (2006) pronouncing a "duty to protect" civilians. Typically U.S. peacekeeping operations are multilateral and United Nations sanctioned. These two elements provide legitimacy.

Other operations with ROE limiting the use of force include stability operations, and anti- and counterterrorist[31] operations, law enforcement, particularly related to drug operations, but also international law related to freedom of navigation and over-flights. The military also participates in the enforcement of sanctions, arms control, rescue and recovery operations, noncombatant evacuation, strikes (political and punitive) and raids (rescue and intelligence gathering), and support to insurgents The President does not secure Congressional consent for many of these operations, but he is likely to consult with, or at least to inform senior members of Congress. The public may or may not have these operations in view.

Gains in surveillance technology have been unprecedented. That technology has been rapidly and broadly adopted by corporations, local and state governments, and, of course, the federal government. Much of that technology has been developed by or for the military and given the United States an enormous advantage over other countries. However, technology can be quickly adopted, and as we can watch our opponents – down to observing the number of people in an automobile in Yemen – so some may soon, or already, be watching us as well. Even if only a limited number of countries have the most advanced surveillance systems, they can share that data as they choose, not just to their own troops, but, for instance, to tribal fighters on the ground. Again, technological advances such as night vision goggles may give demonstrable advantage, but new technology is quickly acquired by others. Thus, there is a technology race comparable to an arms race.

The military's unique action, of course, is the conduct of war.[32]

5 Weapons and capabilities

Nuclear weapons: air, land, and under the sea

Weapons range from hand grenades to nuclear weapons, and capabilities from night vision goggles to skilled computer hacking. It is nuclear weapons, though, which generate the most public debate. Nonproliferation is a central part of U.S. strategy. However, there are already a lot of nuclear weapons spread across the globe. Nine countries have such weapons: North Korea, India, Pakistan, Israel, Britain, France, China, Russia, and the United States. North Korea is thought to have only a few weapons and India, Pakistan and Israel 100 or fewer. It should be noted that Israel does not admit to having such weapons, and that, although North Korea may have only a handful, diplomats worry about that country's erratic decision making, and also about the security of Pakistan's weapons. India has been given special treatment. She has not signed the 1968 Non Proliferation Treaty (NPT) but has been given a waiver to conduct nuclear commerce. Britain, France and China have had nuclear weapons for decades but are thought to have 300 or fewer each. Although both Russia and the United States have greatly downsized their inventory since the height of the Cold War,[1] Russia is estimated to have a current inventory of 12,000, perhaps 5,000 of which are operational.[2] The United States is estimated to have an inventory of fewer than 10,000, 2,500 of them operational, the same number in storage, and about 4,500 scheduled for dismantling. The United States weapons are located in thirteen states and five non-nuclear European countries: Belgium, Italy, Turkey, Germany, and the Netherlands.[3]

Only the U.S. Air Force and the Navy have strategic nuclear weapons.[4] In 2010 sixteen B-2s, the "Stealth" bomber, each one capable of carrying sixteen bombs, and forty-four B-52s, a late 1950s aircraft, each capable of carrying 40 bombs, composed the Air Force's strategic (nuclear) bomber force. In addition, the Air Force controlled some 450 (U.S.) land-based Inter-Continental Ballistic Missiles (ICBMs) capable of reaching around the globe in a matter of minutes.[5] The Navy's 336 Submarine Launched Ballistic Missiles (SLBMs) can be launched from under water. Thus, these weapons are both mobile and well concealed – quite different from land-based silo missiles. The Navy has some fourteen nuclear-powered, nuclear-armed Trident submarines, which can patrol up to ninety days. Each carries twenty-four SLBMs, which are multiply targeted, giving the Navy perhaps 40 percent of U.S. deployed nuclear weapons. Some of these submarines are always on patrol.

The 2010 START calls for a limit of 700 launchers for nuclear warheads. This will require a reduction of almost 150 of existing U.S. launchers. The 1967 Outer Space Treaty, ratified by both the United States and the Soviet Union, forbids nuclear weapons in space.

Primary weapons by service

The Air Force

As of 2010 the Air Force had fifty satellites and more than 5,500 aircraft in service in addition to its 450 silo-located ICBMs.[6] It also has a lot of Unmanned Aerial Vehicles (UAVs),[7] commonly referred to as drones, which will be discussed later. The Active Duty Inventory, which does not include National Guard or Reserve aircraft, consists of 3,322 aircraft in eight categories. Roughly half are in an "active," ready for action, inventory and in the following discussion that is the number which will be used. Remember that a similar number of aircraft are authorized and exist.

There are more than 150 bombers in the active inventory. The newest, the B-2, which looks like a bat and is known as the Spirit or as the Stealth bomber, was first used in the Kosovo War (Figure 5.1). There are fifteen to twenty in service. The cost for an individual B-2

Figure 5.1 The B-2 can penetrate previously impenetrable defenses anywhere in the globe. U.S. Air Force photo by Bobbie Garcia. Source: www. af.mil.

is about $1 billion, which has generated debate about how many are really needed. The oldest bomber, the backbone of the fleet, is the B-52 Stratofortress, a long range (8,800 miles), nuclear-armed aircraft that can fly at an altitude of 50,000 feet. The B-1 Lancer has been operational since 1986, but like the B-52 has been continuously upgraded. There are sixty-seven in operation; each can carry twenty-four tons of bombs. The B-1 is not currently armed with nuclear weapons.

The most numerous aircraft are the fighters. The primary mission for some is air-to-air combat; for others the primary mission is ground attack. They number about 1,500. There are close to 700 F-16 Fighting Falcon dogfighters.[8] Lightweight, with a bubble canopy, the plane travels at a speed of 1,500 mph and with a ferry range of 2,000 miles can, for instance, fly 500 miles, engage in combat, and return to base. Although relatively slow, the plane is a popular export and is flown by some twenty-five countries although it is no longer produced for U.S. use. The newest fighter is the F-22, Raptor, which includes stealth technology (Figure 5.2). Each of the 140 F-22s costs over $143 million.[9] In 2011 Secretary of Defense Robert Gates announced plans to

Figure 5.2 The F-22 Raptor. U.S. Air Force photo by Tech. Sgt. Ben Bloker.
 Source: www.af.mil.

reduce planned acquisitions of F-22s. However, the Navy, Marines, and Air Force are in the process of developing a new fighter, the F-35, known as the Joint Strike Fighter, which will eventually replace the 340 A-10 Thunderbolts or "Warthogs." The oldest fighter, the F-15 and its variants, is still in use by both the United States and a number of allies.

The second largest category is that of a variety of trainers – over a thousand. The third largest category is that of the transport or cargo ("C") aircraft.[10] The 450-plus cargo planes include the C-17 Globemaster, the C-130 Hercules, and the C-5 Galaxy (Figure 5.3). The C-17 has a crew of three and can carry about 170,000 pounds. It can transport tanks and helicopters as well as troops, has an international range, and can land on a short runway. Although the Pentagon had planned to shut down production, Congress has appropriated funds for a total of more than 200 C-17s. The C-130 has been in continuous production since 1954. A versatile plane, but with a range of only some 2,300 miles, it is often used for airdrops. More than 2,000 have been built and they are used by sixty-seven countries. The Galaxy is the largest of the cargo aircraft. Like other planes it has evolved over time.

Tankers keep other aircraft in the air by refueling them. The bulk of the Air Force inventory of 260 tankers are the KC-135s, first developed

Figure 5.3 The C-5 Galaxy. U.S. Air Force photo by Tech. Sgt. Charlie Miller.
Source: www.af.mil.

in the 1950s. In early 2011 the Air Force contracted for a new tanker, Boeing's KC-X, a version of which, the KC 767, is already being flown by several other countries. Each KC-X is estimated to cost over $140 million.

The Air Force has a helicopter fleet of only 150-odd. The aircraft are used for field support and search and rescue missions, and by Special Forces. They include the UH-1 Hueys and the HH-60, the Pave Hawk; the CV-22 is the newest helicopter. A version of the Marines' Osprey (Figure 5.4), it has an extended range and tilt-rotors so the plane can take off vertically and then shift to forward flight. Its unit cost is estimated at over $90 million.

The last aircraft category is Reconnaissance (intelligence collection); it encompasses the high-altitude U-2, the AWACS (E-3), which also has a communications, command, and control function, the E-4, designed as a survivable, mobile command post, and the EC-130, a variant of the Hercules, which has a broadcasting mission for civil affairs and psychological operations. Two OC-135s routinely fly unarmed observation missions in support of the Open Skies Treaty.

Figure 5.4 The CV-22 Osprey. U.S. Air Force photo by Staff Sgt. Markus Maier. Source: www.af.mil.

All of the above and the RC135, which monitors electromagnetic communications, have flight crews. Quite different are the RPVs, also referred to as unmanned aerial vehicles (UAVs). The RQ-4 is a high-altitude and long-endurance RPV that has flown the Pacific, from California to Australia. Much in the news because of their use in Iraq, Afghanistan, and elsewhere in the Middle East are the MQ-1, Predator, and its newer version, the MQ-9, Reaper (Figure 5.5). They began with a surveillance mission that soon expanded to targeted killing and to an attack mission as well. First used in Bosnia in 1995, the MQs can be "flown" by an operator located in Nevada.[11] Other RPVs fly themselves, that is, are launched with a program directing their mission including their return. There is a continuing debate about RPV accuracy, that is, about the ratio of civilian deaths to targeted individuals. There is also a certain amount of angst over the prospect of RPVs filling roles once filled by manned aircraft. That is because the Air Force has always been pilot-centric. The RPVs

Figure 5.5 The MQ9 Reaper. Source: www.af.mil.

reduce the need for cockpit pilots and may make other Air Force bomber and fighter missions less crucial to successful operations. The Predator's unit cost is approximately $4.5 million, the long range Reaper's $10.5 million.

Currently the Air Force controls some fifty satellites: five DMSP meteorological satellites, eight DSCS secure communication satellites, thirty GPS geo-positioning satellites, the new Milstar joint military communications satellite, SBIRS, a space-based infrared system satellite, and WGS, a wideband global satellite.

These systems have combat functions but also important and substantial support functions. They are weapons but also "capabilities" important to "operations other than war" and also to operations that have nothing to do with war. Whereas the United States strives to always be on technology's cutting edge (remember DARPA?), it does not always try to monopolize its technology. Some projects are joint with other countries. Also, the United States may make a profit from military sales to other countries. Sometimes a certain effort at control may be involved, for example, spare parts may not be made available;

this limits the freedom of other countries to use the weapons they have purchased or been given.

It is important to remember that, once a technology is developed, other countries are likely to develop similar technologies. Thus, China was able to develop and display a stealth aircraft in early 2011. It did so during a visit by Secretary Gates, probably partly to express its displeasure over United States' military sales to Taiwan in spite of the U.S. official "one China policy." As a technology becomes widely available, there is an incentive to forge ahead with the development of even newer weapons and capabilities. Such development can take years and billions of dollars. During that time challenges and threats may dramatically shift, but it can be hard to discard or scale back a project once launched – especially if it involves a loss of jobs.

The Army

Guns are basic to the Army, and the M16 assault rifle and its shorter and lighter version, the M4, are the Army's basic assault rifles.[12] The M16 is gas operated with a target range of more than 500 yards and costs about $1,000. The M9 Beretta pistol has been used since 1990. Special Forces often use different weapons from the regular forces, for example the Glock pistol. These weapons are available for sale to civilians.

Machine guns include the light M249 SAW (Squad Automatic Weapon, Figure 5.6), the medium M240, and the heavy M2 machine guns. The last is mounted on a vehicle, a helicopter or a boat, and is also used by the Navy and Air Force, which call it the GAU-17/A. The Special Forces use a compact, versatile and reliable submachine gun called an HK MP5. Machine guns provide rapid fire, for example the SAW can shoot more than 750 rounds a minute at an effective range of 1,000 yards. Its unit cost is estimated at $4,000. Civilians are not allowed to purchase it.

The Army's missiles are the unguided AT 4, which can be launched by a standing individual, the larger, anti-tank guided TOW, the new Javelin, an anti-tank weapon weighing only fifty pounds and launched from the shoulder, and the FIM-92 Stinger, which is an anti-aircraft weapon (Figure 5.7). The TOW has a crew of four and a range of some two miles.[13] Unit replacement is estimated at $180,000.[14] The Javelin

Figure 5.6 The M249, the SAW. Camera Operator LCPL Casey N. Thurston (taken by a marine at a Marine instruction course. Source: www. af.mil.

Figure 5.7 A Stinger missile. Author: Cpl. Adam F. Testagrossa. Source: www.army.mil.

has a shorter range; its cost per unit has been estimated at $125,000 and each missile has been estimated at $40,000 or more. The Army and Marines have an inventory of more than 13,000 Stingers whose unit cost is said to be $25–35,000.

There are four major artillery weapons, also known as cannons or howitzers. These support other units and require a crew to operate. The M119 is easily towed by a humvee or truck and has a range of twelve miles. It takes a crew of five to seven and can fire three rounds a minute for thirty minutes. The larger M198 can also be towed but requires a crew of nine (Figure 5.8). It has a range of over eighteen miles and in short periods can fire four rounds a minute. It is highly accurate and its eighty-five-pound shells have a destruction radius of fifty meters. Its replacement cost is estimated at more than $500,000. The new M777 is replacing the M198. It is lighter and has a greater range, a smaller crew, and a digital fire-control system. In contrast the M109, or Paladin, is not towed. It is a self-propelled, track vehicle cannon. Grenade launchers and mortars are short-range tube weapons, some of which can be carried by a single individual.

Figure 5.8 The M-198 Howitzer. Source: www.army.mil.

Mobility is crucial to the Army; that is why it has helicopters – more than the total number of Air Force aircraft of all kinds. The Apache is an attack helicopter; the Black Hawk is a transport helicopter that has largely replaced the smaller Huey; the venerable, two-rotor Chinook can carry thirty-three troops and up to thirteen tons of cargo; the Kiowa Warrior provides reconnaissance. Unit cost of an Apache is estimated at over $18 million, that of the Blackhawk at about $14 million.

The Army's wheels include the MRAP, Mine Resistant Ambush Protected vehicle; the FMTV, Family of Medium Tactical Vehicles (trucks), some of which can carry 10,000 pounds of cargo and cost about $160,000 each; the HEMTT (Heavy Expanded Mobility Truck), which is the standard cargo truck and can ford four feet of water; the HMMWV (High Mobility Multipurpose Wheeled Vehicle – the Humvee or Hummer), which replaced the jeep; the HET (Heavy Equipment Transporter); the PLS (Palletized Load System); and the 2002 Stryker, which is an armed attack vehicle rather than a cargo

Figure 5.9 The Stryker Mobile Gun System. Author: Jason Kaye. Source: www.army.mil.

vehicle (Figure 5.9). It can travel 60 mph and cover 300 miles on some fifty gallons of gas, and each Stryker costs about $1.5 million.

The Army's tracked vehicles can go where its wheels cannot. Although much modified, the M113 armed personnel carrier is used in more than fifty countries; more than 80,000 have been produced at a unit cost of $41,000. The two commonly thought of as tanks are the Abrams (M1A2), typically used in battle, and the Bradley (M2, M3), a fighting vehicle with bells and whistles such as infrared sensors, a GPS system, digital communications, and more. Its unit cost is more than $3 million. The M88A2 tows, winches, and hoists in fulfilling its mission of recovery.

The Navy

The Navy has just under 300 ships in service.[15] It has more than 3,700 aircraft. Carriers are the Navy's prestige ships. Although few in number they provide a forward presence and can cruise close to the scene of most of the world's trouble spots. There are ten Nimitz class carriers, the largest ships in the world at over 1,000 feet (three football fields) in length. These are manned by a crew of more than 5,500 and carry sixty or more aircraft. There is also one Enterprise class carrier with similar characteristics, which will soon be retired (Figure 5.10). Both are nuclear powered. A Gerald Ford class carrier is being developed, which should be able to carry more than seventy-five aircraft.[16] Including research and development costs it is expected to cost $14 billion.

The Navy's attack submarines are also nuclear powered. Forty-some Los Angeles class, about twenty Ohio class, and a handful of Seawolfs and Virginia class submarines are in service. A "next-generation" attack submarine, the Virginia class, has innovations that permit operations in shallow water and enable Special Forces to leave the sub while it is under water and use Scuba gear or mini-subs to reach nearby land. Periscopes will be replaced with Photonics Masts with high-resolution images and infrared digital cameras. In addition to protecting U.S. ships, these submarines collect intelligence and, importantly, can attack land targets using cruise missiles. The projected cost is $1.8 billion per submarine.

Figure 5.10 The USS *Enterprise*. U.S. Navy photo by Photographers Mate Airman Rob Gaston. Source: www.army.mil.

The ballistic missile submarines (SSBNs), sometimes referred to as "Boomers," were discussed above. They carry Trident nuclear missiles and are specifically designed for long patrols; on average they spend seventy-seven days at sea before returning to port for maintenance.

Guided missile submarines (SSGNs), are four SSBNs converted to become a platform for Special Forces and for land attack. They carry tactical but not strategic (nuclear) missiles.

The Navy's amphibious warfare vessels (referred to as LHA and LHD ships) resemble small carriers but their role is to support a Marine Expeditionary force. Thus, they carry thousands of troops, helicopters, and landing craft including Landing Craft, Air Cushioned (LCACs). Ten are assault ships while another nine specialize in transportation and a dozen called dock landing ships support amphibious landings. LHAs are being refitted to extend their use by fifteen years at a cost of about $1 billion each.

The Navy has about twenty cruisers (Figure 5.11) and some fifty or sixty destroyers. These large surface ships are armed with guided

Figure 5.11 The Guided Missile Cruiser USS *Leyte Gulf*. U.S. Navy photo by
          Mass Communication Specialist Seaman Jared M. King. Source:
          www.army.mil.

missiles and torpedoes. A cruiser's crew typically consists of twenty-
four officers and 340 enlisted personnel; a destroyer's crew is somewhat smaller. They have an undersea, surface, and air mission that is
both defensive and offensive. They typically operate with other ships
in a Strike Force.

Close to thirty frigates are still active although they are in the process of being replaced by Littoral Combat Ships with a variety of missions. The Navy also has tugboats. When the Navy was first ordered
to permit women to serve on ships the tugboat was the Navy's choice
for women.[17]

The F-18 Hornet is the Navy's fighter. It is a single-seat, supersonic,
highly maneuverable jet familiar to many from air shows featuring the
Blue Angels. The Joint Strike Fighter is to replace the earliest version
of the Hornet. It is a variant of the Air Force plane of the same name;
each plane has been estimated to cost $156 million. At one point the
Navy and Air Force combined planned to purchase more than 2,400
of them.

Navy helicopters focus on anti-submarine warfare. So do torpedoes. Another naval weapon is the mine. Important capabilities are advanced radar and sonar.

The Marines

Like the Army, the Marines specialize in land combat after they have been launched from the sea by the Navy. They also have a lot of aircraft. These include some twenty Prowlers, which collect tactical electronic data, 240 Hornet fighters, fifty Hercules cargo planes, and 175 of their own Harrier attack planes. The Marines also fly hundreds of helicopters, some of which are also flown by other services. Some, such as the Sea King and the Super and Sea Stallion, are Marine airships. The CV-22 Osprey (Figure 5.4) is a tilt-rotor helicopter that can take off vertically, but then fly horizontally. Its accidents, expense, and flaws have made it controversial. Nevertheless, the Air Force and Navy are considering its use as well as the Marines. Congress has faithfully supported it even when a Secretary of Defense advised ending its development.

The rifle is nearly sacred to the Marine.[18] The M-16 is the most used, but a total of ten carbines and rifles are listed in the Marine inventory. So what is the big picture? In every instance the United States is better armed than a host of other countries combined. Its advanced technology makes its inventory expensive. However, it sees its mission as not just that of defending the United States proper, but of defending its interests globally, and also playing a significant role in defending many other countries including countries with which it may or not have a treaty. It constructs its reach as global. It expects to be able to have an effect any place in the world. It sees no immediate threat from Latin America or Africa, but, nevertheless, recently created an African command. Currently its strategic thinking focuses on the Middle East, Russia, and China. The next chapter considers the ever-increasing Department of Defense budget; something to remember: the DOD budget has been steadily increasing even when costs for the Afghanistan and Iraq wars are not included.

6   The budget[1]

Overview

It is hard to grasp the size of the Department of Defense (DOD) budget. The 2010 budget request was for 553.8 billion dollars, or $553,800,000,000.[2] Importantly, this was the request for the base budget. The cost of the two wars in which the United States was engaged (Iraq and Afghanistan) was *not* included. An additional $130,000,000,000 was requested for war expenses, referred to as "overseas contingency expenses." Officials expected additional contingency funds would be requested later in the year, which would bring the 2010 total to roughly $700,000,000,000.

There are three points to bear in mind. First, quite apart from the expense of the two wars, the DOD base budget has been steadily increasing over the last decade. Second, U.S. DOD spending is estimated at 40 to 50 percent of the total of all military spending, that is, the spending of all nations combined. Specifically, it is five or six times the size of the military budgets of Russia and also China. Third, DOD's billions make the budgets requested for the State Department, for foreign operations,[3] and for Homeland Security look puny. They were $16.3 billion, $36.7 billion, and $55.1 billion respectively.[4]

Although the perspectives noted above inevitably arise in any discussion of the DOD budget, to determine whether that budget is too large, too small, or as Goldilocks would have said "just right", one must break it down into components and then consider just how particular items fit into U.S. military strategy. Before facing that issue, here are some other ways of thinking about the budget as a whole and also how resources are allocated within the DOD budget.

Some think that the way to think about DOD spending is to consider what percentage of gross domestic product (GDP) goes to defense. At the height of the Cold and Vietnam Wars in the 1960s, DOD spending reached 9 percent of GDP. During the 1970s it slipped to about 5 percent and during the Reagan years increased to 6 percent. After the collapse of the Soviet Union, DOD spending fell, reaching 3 percent of GDP by the end of the 1990s. During George W. Bush's first term, however, it was increased to 4 percent and it is now about 4.5 percent.

O'Hanlon argues that the wars and their costs are visible to the public and debate about both can and does occur. However, he believes that the base budget goes largely unexamined and that waste and unnecessary programs and expenses in that portion of the budget too often go unchallenged. Thus, new technology may be pursued because it is new; war planning may consider remote contingencies; modernization may proceed too rapidly; and estimates of future costs may be ridiculously low. Thus, O'Hanlon says, the issue is not the size of the budget; it is precisely where expenditures are being made and whether they support U.S. strategy. The data shown below are for 2009 base budget requests and are taken from O'Hanlon.

One way to think about allocations is by service department. The 2009 request included:

Army	$139 billion
Navy	$149 billion
Air Force	$144 billion
DOD	$87 billion

Note that the Navy's request includes the Marine Corps and that the Air Force request includes many intelligence assets such as satellites. Again, the total of some $519,000,000,000 does not include costs of the wars.[5]

Another way to look at the budget is to look at categories regardless of service:

Military Personnel	$129 billion[6]
Operations and Maintenance	$180 billion
Procurement	$104 billion
Research, Development, Testing, Evaluation	$80 billion
Military Construction and Family Housing	$24 billion

Still another way of considering DOD expenditures is to break requests down into functions.

Strategic Forces (nuclear)	$10 billion
General Purpose Forces	$202 billion
Mobility Forces (transportation)	$14 billion
Guard and Reserve Forces	$38 billion
Special Operations Forces	$9 billion
Command, Control, Communications	
Intelligence, Space	$78 billion
Research and Development	$53 billion
Central Supply and Maintenance	$22 billion
Training, Medical, Other	$71 billion
Administration	$19 billion
Support of Other Nations	$2 billion

Again, these are base budget requests. Wartime supplementals have been significant. O'Hanlon estimates that by the end of 2008 the Iraq war had already cost $600 billion and Afghanistan $150 billion.[7] Since 2008 the United States has surged in Iraq and is increasing counterinsurgency efforts in Afghanistan. It is now estimated that the costs per deployed U.S. troop is more than $400,000 per year.[8]

Still another way to think about base budget allocations is to divide it by geographic region. One clearly outdated estimate saw 34 percent of the budget as directed toward Central and Northern Europe, 20 percent toward the Middle East and the Persian Gulf, 15 percent toward strategic nuclear deterrence, 12 percent toward maintaining sea lanes in the Atlantic and Pacific, 6 percent toward South Korea, and a similar amount to national intelligence and communications.[9]

A final way to think about the budget is to estimate the cost (and therefore the savings if eliminated) of particular military units. For example, O'Hanlon uses an estimate of $5 billion as the cost of each Active Army Division, $3 billion for an Active Air Force Tactical Air Wing, and $6.4 billion for a Navy Carrier Battle Group. The point is: a particular goal can often be achieved in a variety of ways and one way may be substantially cheaper than another. For example, using B-52 bombers, which are cheaper but carry fewer bombs, may be cheaper than using B-2s – or maybe not. The calculation can and should be done rather than simply dividing up the mission or assuming newer is better. More contentious might be a decision that the savings from eliminating one Navy Carrier Battle Group would more than pay for an Army Division, the currently most overworked element in the military.[10]

The most obvious way to cut costs is to reduce the purchase of expensive planes and ships, but even greater savings might come from assessing the most economic way to fulfill particular U.S. commitments – or even to rethink those commitments.[11] Similarly, logistics costs should be examined. One estimate is that it takes a ton of supplies a day for every ten soldiers in an overseas operation. That cost should be considered versus overseas basing.[12] Such analyses can be complex, but they are the kind experts should be making and citizens should be debating.

At bottom the question is: what, precisely, is needed to defend the country? The answer should be derived from an analysis of the threat or threats to the United States and the consequent development of a strategic plan to counter them. Should be. Remember the QDR? It contained a lengthy list of threats including even such things as global warming. It also assumed a rather large umbrella for the protection of "allies and partners." Again, the time may have come to be explicit and limited in defining threats. Having done so, military spending could then reflect specific strategies designed to reduce or eliminate those threats. Spending directed toward threats that are no longer critical, or spending that simply seeks "global dominance" could then be eliminated. So could spending on a variety of threats mentioned in the QDR that do not necessarily require a military response, items such as global warming or a failing food supply. No explicit and concrete strategy currently exists. Allocations are, nevertheless, made. Much of the current debate focuses on efforts to rein in procurement. Cuts in that part of the budget, however, are likely to involve job losses and, therefore, Congressional resistance. Remember that Congress provides the resources and sometimes it actually gives DOD more than it has requested.

Procedures and allocations

The formulation of the military budget begins in the Department of Defense. The DOD's request is then shaped by the President's Office of Management and the Budget (OMB), which prepares the President's formal budget request. This is delivered to Congress at the beginning of February. Congressional work on what is called the National Defense Authorization Act involves (1) consideration by the subcommittees of the House and Senate Armed Services committees and then by the full committees, (2) passage of a budget resolution by each house, (3) the reconciliation of differences between the resolutions of the two houses by a conference committee with members from both houses, (4) passage of the agreed upon bill by each house, and (5) a presidential signature. This is not the whole story, however. There is a whole second review by the Defense Subcommittees of the two houses' Appropriations Committees. Money "authorized" cannot be spent until it is "appropriated." The legislative process that begins in February is supposed to be completed by October 1 because this is when the federal fiscal year begins. However, a stopgap spending measure becomes necessary if the process is not completed by October. The DOD budget must be passed annually. Moreover, it is "discretionary," not mandated, and funds cannot be committed beyond two years.[13]

Many are involved in shaping the DOD request. This includes officers working for their services, officers and civilians working for the Secretary of Defense, contractors to DOD, and even "volunteers" at think tanks and universities who sometimes prepare their own recommendations. Faculty, staff, even students at the War Colleges and the staff of the Joint Chiefs contribute as well. In the early stages participants are likely to focus on their own positions and interests; they are even likely to game the system by asking for "more," expecting that whatever they ask for will be reduced as the process continues.

The Pentagon's formal process known as PPBE involves planning, programming, budgeting and execution. Planning is supposed to be based on the Pentagon's National Military Strategy, which is based on the President's National Security Strategy.[14] It is at the programming stage that specifics emerge as the services and agencies develop program objective memoranda (POMs). They do so with budget ceilings set by the OMB. Using the POMs the Office of the Secretary of Defense then forges a Future Years Defense Program (FYDP), a five-year program. Note, though, that detail is provided only for the first two years, and Congress appropriates funds only for the first year.

The Congressional Budget Office (CBO), which includes a set of defense experts, plays an important role in translating the DOD budget request for use by legislators, the media, and the public. It has been particularly attentive to estimating costs of large ticket items such as planes, ships, and missiles.

The military budget is contained in the National Defense Authorization Act. Like all federal budget legislation it originates in the House of Representatives. Before it reaches the floor of the House for a vote it has been vetted by the House Armed Services Committee and its subcommittees. When Republican Buck McKeon became chair of that committee in 2011 he reorganized the subcommittees. There are seven committees: Tactical Air and Land Forces, Seapower and Projection Forces, Strategic Forces, Emerging Threats and Capabilities, Military Personnel, Readiness, and Oversight and Investigation. In addition there is a Defense Acquisition Reform Panel.

The Senate follows a similar procedure. Unsurprisingly, committee members of both houses are intensively lobbied by the defense industry. What may be surprising is that the services can be described as lobbying too. The services are represented to the Congress by DOD,[15] but because Congress is constitutionally responsible for the common defense by raising and supporting armies and by providing and maintaining a navy (see Article I Section 8) it is the military's second boss. When Congress calls for testimony from military officers those officers can be caught between providing their best judgment and supporting the views of their superiors at DOD.

There is a good deal of interaction between the service committees and their staff and military leadership. In fact, each service maintains a liaison office, which is well staffed and led by an admiral or a general. There is a nexus, then, between Congress, the military, and corporations that profit from military contracts. Former General Dwight D. Eisenhower warned about the influence of what he called "the military–industrial complex" in his Farewell Address to the nation some fifty years ago. That complex, which includes the Congress, is alive and well but it has recently changed in a significant way.

Contracts and outsourcing

Again, major defense contractors invest millions in Congressional campaigns every two years; retired military officers become corporate officers and lobbyists; large numbers of well-paid workers are employed in the defense industry; and defense contracts can be large. In 2009 the top contractors had contracts worth billions. Specifically they were:

Lockheed Martin	$12,000,000,000
Northrop Grumman	$9,000,000,000
Boeing	$8,000,000,000
Raytheon	$6,000,000,000
General Dynamics	$5,000,000,000
KBR, Inc.	$4,500,000,000
Science Applications	$4,000,000,000

Contracting for supplies and equipment is an old story and there have always been complaints of waste and "profiteering." Further, some contracts have been specifically written for "cost plus profit."[16] What is new is widespread contracting for services that in the past were performed by the military.

One important reason for this is that after the collapse of the Soviet Union the United States cut military personnel by 25 percent. However, it did not cut back on operations. In fact, by 2010 it was engaged in two long-distance wars. The result is that troops are seeing multiple tours in combat zones, Guard and Reserve troops are not being held in reserve but are regularly activated and sent abroad, and the military is hiring a lot of people to do jobs once done by those in uniform. In fact, in Iraq there has been one contract employee for every American in uniform. Only a fifth of those contractors were U.S. citizens, some of whom were retired military. Two fifths were Iraqis. The remaining two fifths were brought in from other countries, many of them in low-wage jobs.

The use of contract employees as cooks evoked little clamor. It is the use of contractors as security personnel, as prison guards, as interrogators and spies that has created a stir.[17] Some would describe at least some of the contract workers as mercenaries, soldiers for hire, a concept that has had a bad name ever since Machiavelli wrote *The Art of War* and German mercenaries fought for England in the U.S. War for Independence.[18]

The legal standing and liability of contract workers in Iraq has been a matter of dispute.

In 2007 all Americans associated with the American government had immunity from prosecutions based on Iraqi law. The most recent status of forces agreement (SOFA) has changed that. Since 2007 the Uniform Code of Military Justice (UCMJ) has made persons accompanying armed forces (for example, embedded journalists) subject to the UCMJ. This may sound like double jeopardy; in fact, the perception is the opposite: it is that contract employees often can act with impunity. The best-known providers of contract workers are KBR, Booze, Allen and Hamilton, and Xe, formerly known as Blackwater.[19] Some argue that using contractors can cut costs for overseas operations by up to 50 percent. This may make sense if locals can provide needed services and is probably true in the case, for instance, of interpreters. On the other hand, there has been dismay over the fact that some highly trained members of the U.S. military retire and then go to work for a contractor at an exponentially higher salary. In the latter instance, an individual might make thousands every week, but, of course, the gig could be short-lived.

Military sales

The Department of Defense has a large sales program.[20] Arms and services can also be purchased directly from corporations. In both cases, however, sales are subject to approval by the Department of State and the U.S. Congress, and, of course, export laws. Some DOD sales make a profit for the department; some sales are paid for by a grant – from the DOD. Apart from profit and from reducing the unit cost of, say, a jet fighter, sales can help to strengthen the U.S. military's relationship with another country's military. This can enhance future 'interoperability"; it can also link the United States to a military whose actions it may sometimes deplore.

It may not be a surprise to learn that the United States, which spends the most on its military, also sells the most arms. In 2009 it agreed to \$31,682,000,000 in total arms sales and delivered \$12,726,000,000 worth of arms.[21] Many of those sales have been to developing countries; among them Saudi Arabia, India, the UAE, Egypt, and Pakistan. Sometimes sales have been to both sides of a dispute, for example to Pakistan and India and to Egypt and Israel.[22]

Since the 2001 attack on the World Trade Center, restrictions based on human rights violations have been lifted for some countries, for example Indonesia. A particularly tricky issue concerns Taiwan, which has made major purchases from the United States presumably to defend itself against China, which claims it as a province. This is in spite of the U.S. "One China' policy and formal recognition of the People's Republic of China (PRC).[23] Recently the DOD proposed more than \$4,000,000,000 in sales to rearm Iraq including F-16 aircraft.[24] In 2010 it was discussing a \$60,000,000,000 package for Saudi Arabia including fighters and Black Hawk helicopters and was also discussing a possible \$30,000,000,000 investment in Saudi naval facilities.[25]

Debates about U.S. arms sales usually emphasize expensive, high-tech weaponry. It should be remembered, however, that the small arms trade is also a matter of international concern. Simply equipped forces have had significant success against the United States in Afghanistan; in other parts of the world there have been numerous low-tech conflicts, some of them murderous and long enduring, for example in Sudan.

The black budget

The black budget is one of those anomalies in a democracy, a budget for items to be kept secret not just from an enemy, not just from the American people, but from many, if not most, of their Congressional representatives as well – sometimes even from Armed Service and/or Intelligence Committee members. Both the DOD and the Central Intelligence Agencies have black budgets. Analysts believe that the DOD black budget is somewhere between $55,000,000,000 and $60,000,000,000. This is adduced by adding items labeled "classified programs" to the sums budgeted under a code name. The total is roughly 10 percent of the department's base budget.

The black budget can go to the research and procurement of advanced weapons such as the Stealth bomber. It can also go to secret operations, which are typically carried out by Special Forces units. The CIA also conducts secret operations, and there is some ambiguity about defining such operations and some discussion about their legality. There is a distinction between a clandestine operation, which is a normal but secret military operation, and a covert operation. The military describes the first as legal because it is routine, supports traditional military activities, and is "passive" in the pursuit of intelligence. It argues that participants would be protected under the Geneva Conventions as acting under military orders and that Congress does not have to be notified. "Active," covert operations are not only secret, but their legality requires a written presidential "finding" and the notification of Congressional intelligence committees. The standing of covert operators under the Geneva Conventions is not clear. Although the CIA has engaged in a large number and variety of covert operations since its 1947 founding, Congress has expressed some concern that, since the World Trade Center attack and the expansion of Special Forces, the military may more and more be engaging in the kind of covert actions traditionally associated with the CIA, for example targeted assassinations. Whereas this is already a Congressional concern, it is also the kind of policy issue that could be a concern to citizens.

7 Policy questions

The purpose of this book has been to provide a primer to "arm" readers for debates/discussions about the proper nature and use of national militaries, particularly the U.S. military. It has not aspired to be a desk reference that could provide an answer to any or even most questions. It does, though, seek to provide information about where readers can find answers to questions they may have. Note especially the section following this chapter for a substantial, but hardly inclusive, list of resources.

There are myriad issues worthy of discussion. Most will be deferred for now. Those which are complex and/or technical will require more information if one is to develop a well-founded position about them. However, there are a set of issues which the reader may want to begin to consider now. Several are outlined below.

The first is: what is a vital national interest and what is merely a national interest? Is the "interest" that of the government, that of the economy, that of the citizenry? What time frame is relevant: the next year, five years, ten years, twenty years? And, importantly, is the military the best way to protect a particular interest?

Second, is there a "responsibility to protect"? This has elements of the aristocratic *noblesse oblige*, that is, privilege/power entails responsibility. There are two rather different contexts. One involves the duty one has to a range of formal and informal commitments made to "partners and allies." In this case the question is not only whether the commitments are appropriate, but also whether they will actually be fulfilled, or even if they *can* be fulfilled. The second case is rather different and has been promoted more recently, in particular, in the case of Libya's suppression of insurgents. In this context the principle asserts a responsibility to intervene if a government or an (un)civil conflict is likely to end in something akin to the massacre/ genocide in Rwanda in 2004. The event that may have first sparked discussion about a responsibility to protect was the 1995 massacre in Srebrenica where UN peacekeepers fulfilled their mission, which was limited to observation, when there was a possibility that they might have intervened to prevent the carnage. There are several issues. One is that no one invokes this responsibility when the bad behavior is that of a powerful or even semi-powerful state, such as Zimbabwe. Nor is it clear who should intervene. Those who are nearby and able? Only a military that is authorized, for instance, by the United Nations? Only an international force?

Further, a "responsibility to protect" runs head-on into the concept of sovereignty. This has been a fundamental principle underpinning the United Nations. It has also been a jealously guarded principle of the United States as demonstrated by its failure to ratify a variety of United Nations conventions. Examples include the Convention to Eliminate Discrimination against Women, the Convention on the Law of the Sea, and the Convention on the Rights of the Child.[1] The United States has actually helped shape some conventions that it has then not ratified. It should be noted that in the United States there are two steps. The first is a signature by the president. The second is ratification by the Senate by a two-thirds vote. Sometimes the President will sign a convention but then not submit it to a Senate vote, where it would surely fail. The Senate's position is firmly rooted in the principle of not limiting U.S. sovereignty in any way. Often it is noted that there is some hypocrisy involved on the part of other nations which do sign, but do so only with formal reservations or even with no intention whatsoever of implementing the convention.[2]

Another topic, then, would be the degree to which a country such as the United States adheres to international law even if it does not acknowledge being bound by it. Similarly, accepted ethical standards might not be binding, but the United States may choose to act in accordance with them. This may be because it agrees with the law/ standards but is wary of compromising its sovereignty, or it may honor an international norm simply for pragmatic reasons – because it gains international respect by doing so.

There are a number of issues related to the relationship between citizens and their military. The overall topic is referred to as "civil–military relations". Occasionally, there is a conflict between what senior military officers may consider their professional obligation and their duty to the President, their Commander in Chief. Another issue relates to the representativeness of the military. Should it look more like the citizenry? Or is it sufficient to say that there are no categorical exclusions from the military or from particular assignments in the military? The U.S. military has not had exclusions based on race or ethnicity for more than half a century. Women are now permitted to serve except in Special Forces and ground combat units, although the latter policy is under review. Further, the U.S. military has recently removed the barrier to service once imposed against gays and lesbians. Again, exclusions are nearly ended, but one variable remains. The U.S. military is very middle-class. Few members of the upper class choose to serve.[3] Similarly, low-income young men and women are also not represented. This is not just a matter of choice. Many are ineligible for lack of education, for being unfit, or for possessing a criminal record.

A final issue concerns retired officers, particularly very senior officers. Do they become ordinary citizens or should they constrain themselves or be constrained from participating directly in politics, from lobbying, from working for defense contractors? When Bill Clinton ran for President, he organized an endorsement by a group of retired senior officers. Since then at least one such officer has addressed a presidential nominating convention. Some time ago some officers were so leery of the political that they chose to not even vote. Again, the active political participation of senior retired officers is new and should be examined.[4]

As you begin your own consideration of things military the following section should be of some help.

8 Some resources for more information

There is a great deal of information available on the web. In this section I have selected a variety of sources but the list is by no means exhaustive. Generally, I have described the organizations below as they describe themselves. Also, the organizations may produce reports in a variety of other fields and may have other functions such as advancing policy positions as well as providing research.

Research organizations

American Enterprise Institute for Public Policy Research (AEI): Founded in 1943, this conservative, nonpartisan think tank's mission is to "defend the principles and improve the institutions of American freedom and democratic capitalism."

Brookings Institute: Founded in 1927 but originating in the reform movement of 1916, this institute is committed to conducting independent research and recommendations to advance democracy, the economic and social welfare, security, and opportunity of all Americans, and an open, safe, prosperous, and cooperative international system.

Center for Defense Information (CDI): This center has provided expert analysis on national security, international security, and defense policy since 1972, when its focus was on nuclear weapon; it offers an interesting ebook titled "The Pentagon Labyrinth." It takes no policy positions and no money from the U.S. government.

Center for Naval Analysis (CNA): This decades-old research organization covers a number of fields other than the military.

Center for Strategic and International Studies (CSIS): Admiral Arleigh Burke was one of the founders of CSIS in 1962. Former Senator Sam Nunn is chair of its Board of Trustees. Its focus is defense and security, regional stability, and transnational challenges. It has a staff of over 200 as well as a number of affiliated scholars.

Council on Foreign Relations: This think tank and publisher of *Foreign Affairs* does research but takes no institutional positions. It has an active education program and has sought to link the government, business, and university communities since 1921.

Federation of American Scientists (FAS): Founded in 1945 by scientists associated with building the first atomic bomb and originally devoted to the prevention of nuclear war, FAS is now committed to "evidence-based" research and practical policy recommendations in several areas including bio and strategic security and earth systems.

Heritage Foundation: The mission of the Heritage Foundation is research and education to formulate and promote conservative public policies including national defense. It targets policy makers, the news media, and academia and has begun a Leadership for America Campaign and a Young Leaders Program.

Rand Corporation (RAND): Originally an Air Force project at the Douglas Aircraft Company, RAND became independent in 1948. It offers a PhD in policy analysis and provides research in many areas. Three of its centers are federally funded and it contracts for research with a variety of clients. A portion of its work is classified.

Stockholm International Peace Research Institute (SIPRI): Since 1966 SIPRI has provided research on conflict, armaments, arms control, and disarmament. Its scope is global and its annual yearbook is now available on line as well as in print.

Websites

Army Research Institute, www.hqda.army.mil/ari/: This institute produces a large number of studies every year emphasizing the behavioral and social sciences.

Air Force Research Institute, www.afri.au.af.mil/: The Institute is a part of the Air University. It has a press and publishes the *Strategic Studies Quarterly* and *Air & Space Power*.

Center for Naval Warfare Studies, www.usnwc.edu/Departments-Colleges/Center-for-Naval-Warfare-Studies.aspx: The Center is the research arm of the Naval War College. It includes the Naval War College Press. The College also publishes the *Naval War College Review*.

Defense Technical Information Center, www.dtic.mil: Another source of reports on a range of subjects. Has a new search engine.

Department of Defense, www.defense.gov: This website contains a wealth of information including DOD 101, a primer on DOD. It also lists an additional sixteen DOD websites including the four service websites listed below.

Global Security, www.globalsecurity.org/: Global Security was founded in 2000 to provide both background and breaking news about defense, space, intelligence, and WMD. It is updated hourly and supported in part with ads on its site.

HIS Jane's Defense & Security Intelligence & Analysis, www.janes.com/: This website offers a global perspective. Its fantastic database requires a subscription for full use.

Military One Source, www.militaryonesource.com: An official government website.

Strategic Studies Institute, www.ssi.army/mil: Located at the Army War College, the Institute regularly publishes studies on a range of topics.

Truman National Security Project, www.trumanproject.org: The purpose of this institute is to train a "new generation of progressives."

It is always useful to examine and compare the official sites of each service. They are:

U.S. Air Force, www.airforce.mil
U.S. Army, www.army.mil
U.S. Navy, www.navy.mil
U.S. Marines, www.usmc.mil

Periodicals

The journals below are official government publications.

Air and Space Power
Joint Force Quarterly
Marine Corps Gazette
Naval War College Review
Parameters
Stars and Stripes (which has a First Amendment guarantee)
Strategic Studies Quarterly

These journals and newspapers are independent of the government.

Armed Forces and Society
Defense News
Jane's Defense Weekly
Journal of Military History
Journal of Political and Military Sociology
Military Times and also *Air Force, Army, Marines and Navy Times*
Proceedings (U.S. Naval Institute)

Books

Each of the services has a list of recommended professional reading.[1] Looking at those lists is interesting. The first list below is a "starter list." The second list is more probing.

List 1

The Accidental Guerrilla, David Kilcullen: formulates a new counterinsurgency strategy.

Black Hawk Down, Mark Bowden: A journalist's account of the 1993 battle in which U.S. forces attempted to capture the Somalian warlord Mohamed Adid but lost a Black Hawk helicopter. Also made into a film.

Dispatches, Michael Heer: War correspondent for *Esquire* magazine, Heer gives a visceral account of those doing the fighting in Vietnam.

Fields of Fire, James Webb: A novel about three marines fighting in Vietnam. Webb served in combat in Vietnam and later as Secretary of the Navy. He is currently a Senator from Virginia.

The Limits of Power, Andrew J. Bacevich: A former officer and a conservative, the author provides a sober and realistic view of American power.

Making the Corps, Thomas Ricks: A journalist's account of Marine basic training in 1995, which illustrates the special *esprit* of the corps. His later *Fiasco* covers the Iraq war.

The Masks of War, Carl H. Builder: A 1989 book which delineates the cultural differences between the Army, Navy, and Air Force.

The Military Balance, published by the International Institute for Strategic Studies: appraises the military strength of some 170 countries.

They Marched into Sunlight: War and Peace, Vietnam and America, October, 1967, David Maraniss: Another journalist who compares the antiwar movement at home and troops fighting in Vietnam. Also a film.

We Were Soldiers Once, LTG Harold G. Moore and Joseph L. Galloway: Also a film, this is an account of the large-scale battle of Vietnam's Ia Drang Valley. A West Point graduate with a distinguished career, Moore retired as a Lieutenant General.

What We Know about Army Families, a 2007 report prepared for the Family and Morale, Welfare and Recreation Command.

There is also an "Officer's Guide" for each of the services with wonderful summaries of the officer's role and duties. Recommended – but remember, most military personnel are enlisted.

List 2

Blueprint for Action: Thomas P. M. Barnett reflects on appropriate strategy in a changing and chaotic post-9/11 world.

Citizens and Soldiers: The Dilemmas of Military Service: Eliot Cohen examines the decision to maintain a large military without a draft.

Choosing Your Battles: American Civil–Military Relations and the Use of Force: P. D. Feaver and Christopher Gelpi publish regularly and thoughtfully on the topic.

The Ethics of War, edited by Richard Sorabji and David Rodin: considers the issue from a variety of perspectives and ranges over the centuries.

Gender and International Security: Feminist Perspectives: editor Laura Sjoberg offers a set of not usual views.

Nemesis: The Last Days of the American Republic: Chalmers Johnson severely critiques the gap between America's professed ideals and its actions.

The Professional Soldier, Morris Janowitz: A veteran of World War II, sociologist Janowitz was a founder of the journal *Armed Forces and Society*. This classic is the starting point for thinking about civil–military relations.

Science of War, Michael O'Hanlon: A new book by a Brookings Institute scholar, which is not about science but about critical analysis. It especially examines budget issues.

Soldier and the State, Samuel P. Huntington: Military veteran and political scientist, Huntington in his 1957 classic sees the military as a profession.

Virtual War: Michael Ignatieff uses the Kosovo conflict to explore the meaning of fighting by remote control.

Films

7 Days in May: This 1964 film concerns a military coup in the United States.

Battle of Algiers: A classic account of the 1954–62 war for Algeria's independence. A lesson in insurgency and counterinsurgency.

Band of Brothers: A ten-part HBO miniseries based on historian Stephen E. Ambrose's book by the same title following a company's participation in World War II.

Carrier: A ten-part PBS series depicting a deployment on the USS *Nimitz*.

Flags of Our Fathers: Film based on a volume telling the stories of the five Americans who raised the American flag on Iwo Jima during World War II.

The Fog of War: Eleven Lessons Learned from the Life of Robert S. McNamara: A documentary about the Secretary of Defense during the Vietnam War who later had regrets.

Full Metal Jacket: A film based on a novel titled *The Short-Timers* about a platoon of marines as they trained and then fought in Vietnam.

Glory: A film about an all-African-American volunteer regiment from Massachusetts that fought in the U.S. Civil War.

The Hurt Locker: A 2008 film about a three-person Explosive Ordnance Disposal (EOD) team during the current Iraq war.

Letters from Iwo Jima: The flip side of *Flags of Our Fathers*, this film tells the story of Iwo Jima from the point of view of Japanese soldiers fighting there.

Restrepo: A feature-length documentary about a U.S. platoon fighting in one of the deadliest valleys in Afghanistan.

Tora! Tora! Tora!: A popular dramatization of the attack on Pearl Harbor, which began World War II for most Americans.

Top Gun: Another popular film depicting the life of a reckless jet fighter pilot hero.

Conclusion

There is no conclusion. The intent of this book was only to provide basic information so that readers could begin to draw their own conclusions. Although a few issues were raised, many questions remain – serious ones. Most of them will require more information than has been offered here, but readers should now be ready both to formulate their own questions and to uncover the information needed to answer them. Forge on!

Notes

1 Introduction

1 De facto declarations and the War Powers Act will be discussed later.
2 It should be noted that, even when there is a war, only a limited portion of the military directly participates in it. This varies by service and specialty and with the kind of conflict
3 Some activities which one might imagine are "military" are, in fact, conducted by the Central Intelligence Agency (CIA), whose budgets and activities are far less visible.

2 The A, B, Cs

1 As the conflicts in Iraq and Afghanistan have made clear, one is not necessarily safe because one is in support. Further, when personnel are needed, they are called. Thus, both Air Force and Navy personnel have been assigned to work in Army units in the Middle East.
2 Builder, Carl. *The Masks of War*. Baltimore: Johns Hopkins Press, 1989, p. 5.
3 Its everyday uniform is currently evolving from the familiar dark green to what some consider a more attractive blue.
4 See the Goldwater–Nichols Act. Note also that Joint Forces Command was abolished in late 2011.
5 Huntington, Samuel P. *The Soldier and the State*. New York: Vintage, 1957, ch. 3.
6 Stiehm, Judith. "The Civilian Mind" in *It's Our Military Too!* Philadelphia: Temple University Press, 1996, ch. 13.
7 These data and those on the Reserves are taken from Public Law 110-417, Title IV, sec. 401, 411, and 412, the Duncan Hunter Defense Authorization Act for Fiscal Year 2009. www.dod.mil/dodgc/ok/docs/2009NDAA_PL 110-417.pdf, accessed January 10, 2010.
8 More recently DOD civilians and contractors are also being described as part of the Total Force.

9   www.stripes.com/article.asp?section=104&article=63422, accessed January 21, 2010.

10 It is not always easy to get out of the military. During the Iraq and Afghanistan conflicts the DOD enforced a "stop loss" policy which kept thousands of troops on active duty past the terms of their enlistment contracts. There is also current litigation on behalf of some officers who have not been allowed to resign even though previous rules would have permitted them to do so.

11 Civilians with military technical specialties but who have an unrelated civilian occupation may require some time to bring their skills up to speed.

12 *New York Times*, September 2, 2009.

13 Stiehm, Judith. "The Challenge of Civil–Military Cooperation in Peacekeeping." *Airman Scholar*, Winter 1998, Vol. IV, No. 1, pp. 26–35.

14 P.A. Stinson has prepared a helpful PowerPoint presentation from Department of Defense Manpower Data Center data. See slideshare.net/pastinson/us-military-active-duty-demographic-profile-presentation?from=share_email. Other data are from Shanea Watkins and James Sherk's *Who Serves in the Military? Demographics of Enlisted Troops and Officers*. Washington, DC: Heritage Foundation, 2008. The best single source is "Demographics 2009, Profile of the Military Community" published by the Deputy Under Secretary of Defense (Military Community and Family Policy), which is available only on the web (www.militaryhomefront. dod.mil/12038/Project%20Documents/MilitaryHOMEFRONT/QOL%20 Resources/Reports/2009_Demographics_Report.pdf).

15 A number of enlisted earn associate and even bachelor degrees.

16 Standards for enlistment can be waived when recruiting is difficult. Some media reports in 2011 stated that 75 percent of young people were ineligible for military service. That was incorrect.

17 Officers of equal rank need not salute. Enlisted personnel do not salute each other.

18 That is roughly half the total of Regular, active duty, forces.

19 The Libyan campaign has provoked discussion of the War Powers Resolution of 1973 designed to check an impetuous president. Passed over the veto of President Richard Nixon, the Act requires the President (1) to consult the Congress "in every possible instance" before deploying troops abroad, (2) to report to both houses within 48 hours and periodically about the circumstances and estimated duration of a deployment, and (3) importantly, to terminate deployment within sixty days of the initial report unless Congress specifically approves, or the President requests a thirty-day extension to protect the safety of personnel. Congress also is authorized to direct withdrawal at any time by concurrent resolution, a resolution the President cannot veto. Congress has never invoked the termination clause. Further, although the Supreme Court has not specifically considered the constitutionality of the War Powers Act, it has clearly rejected the concept

of a "legislative veto." It should also be noted that covert operations that do not involve U.S. military forces (typically involving CIA personnel instead) are not covered by the legislation.

20 The code is "uniform" because it applies to all the services. It was adopted in 1951.

21 A General Courts Martial usually involves a judge and five other members while a Special Courts Martial involves a judge and three other members; a Summary Courts Martial may involve only a judge. The last two courts have limited jurisdiction. Judges must be lawyers. In most cases a two thirds vote is sufficient for conviction.

22 Helicopter pilots are an example of a warrant officer, although some helicopter pilots are regular officers.

23 In addition to rates the Navy has ratings, which designate specialties. When the Air Force refers to a "rated" officer it means a pilot or navigator.

24 A description of the range of specialties will be offered below.

25 The Army is in the process of changing to blue uniforms with a white shirt.

26 Although troops have an extensive wardrobe, what they wear on any particular day and for any particular activity is prescribed.

27 Battle dress uniforms are the same for officers and enlisted and for men and women.

28 It may be useful to refer back to Figure 2.1.

29 Battalions and larger units will typically include these elements: (1) administration, (2) intelligence, (3) plans, operations, and training, and (4) logistics.

30 The Army is currently making many changes in its MOS codes.

31 Remember that an individual's "rate" is his pay grade.

32 E-1 through E-3 have only rates. Ratings begin at E-4.

33 www.persnet.navy.mil/ReferenceLibrary/NOC, accessed March 17, 2010.

34 Since 9/11, survivors and dependents have been made eligible for educational assistance as well.

3 Strategy, doctrine, tactics, and skills

1 Strategy, doctrine, and tactics are well-known concepts among military analysts. It should be noted, though, that, in order to emphasize the breadth of strategy, to include diplomacy and economics many analysts now use a formula that begins with "grand strategy," then descends to theater or military strategy, then operational art and, finally, tactics.

2 By law the President is required to provide such a strategy annually. In fact, Bush published only two, and Obama published his first NSS in May 2010 (President Barack Obama, "The National Security Strategy", Washington, DC, May 2010; www.whitehouse.gov/sites/default/files/rss_viewer/national_security_strategy.pdf).

3 There is also now a National Defense Strategy (NDS) prepared by the Secretary of Defense to provide guidance to those preparing the NMS and the Quadrennial Defense Review (QDR). "The National Military Strategy of the United States of America, 2011: Redefining America's Military Leadership," Washington, DC, February 2011, can be found on the website of the Joint Chiefs of Staff (www.jcs.mil). The "Quadrennial Defense Review Report," Washington, DC, February 2010, is posted on the Department of Defense website (www.defense.gov).

4 Including second- and even third-order consequences.

5 In the introduction the NMS warns of the peril of underestimating the stresses of sustained combat on our equipment and people; at the same time it warns potential adversaries of the peril of underestimating U.S. military strength and will.

6 It also includes criminal networks.

7 This topic has not been a part of previous Pentagon calculations.

8 Note that, when the 2011 "upheaval" occurred in Egypt, Egyptian military officials were actually visiting the Pentagon. The nature of military-to-military relations is a largely unexplored policy issue.

9 This is also a new item.

10 Able to act anywhere in any way. Again, though, it is stressed that deterrence also involves diplomacy and economic initiatives. In theory economic initiatives refer to economic development but a substantial amount of U.S. funding may be funneled off by elites or intentionally given to them and/or their militaries.

11 And Taiwan is the trip cord.

12 This is known as the three "d" approach. Secretary of State Hillary Clinton has been its strong proponent.

13 A fourth goal is to preserve and enhance the All-Volunteer Force (AVF) by reforming how business is done and by taking care of our troops. "Taking care" issues include treating post traumatic stress disorder (PTSD).

14 The United States is extremely sensitive to any violation of its own sovereignty. Also, the United Nations has been chary of violating sovereignty. However, the concept of the "responsibility to protect" is gaining support. This would justify intervening if a nation were engaged in acts against its own population such as ethnic cleansing.

15 The training of local police to western standards seems to be a significantly difficult task.

16 The QDR does suggest that some items, for example, the F-22, which was needed when the Soviet Union was a threat, are no longer required in the quantity once planned.

17 The QDR includes some mystifying language, for instance, "consequence management response forces." This refers to personnel such as police and firemen who respond to a disaster and then "manage" its consequences.

18 The principle is not ironclad and it seems certain that in a significant emergency the military would be used and propriety would be assessed

afterwards. The National Guard, though, can be mobilized by a governor to enforce the law.

19 The new Counterinsurgency Field Manual will be discussed below.

20 After the collapse of the Soviet Union, Foreign Area Officers (FAOs) found they were no longer a priority. Only recently has the importance of being able to speak directly with allies and, importantly, with foes again been seen as important.

21 Critical capabilities may mean weapons, but they may also include the sharing of surveillance and intelligence data, and certain technologies.

22 Others argue that a forward posture can be provocative. Thus, Al Qaeda was allegedly created in response to the stationing of U.S. troops in Saudi Arabia even though the troops were welcomed by that government.

23 The cyberspace division of labor between the services and between the military and civilian agencies has not been resolved.

24 This force would be composed of civilians working directly for DOD. It would reduce the number of contractors being employed.

25 It involves decisions about when to use nuclear weapons and what to target. Both its focus and its name change with circumstances and the administration.

26 The next largest arsenal, that of China, is thought to contain fewer than 200 bombs.

27 The United States' priority is its own security, then that of allies and partners. Global stability, though, may require that those outside these parameters also feel secure, that is, have the means to defend themselves – even against us!

28 It is important to know that doctrine is always described as only a guide, one that requires judgment in application. Doctrine does not involve regulations. It does not oblige. Nevertheless, one does not often transgress it.

29 https://asc.army.mil/docs/transformative/Army_Doctrine_Update_FM501_FM30.pdf (2007). Further, it was directed that analysis of the environment include Political, Military, Economic, Social, Infrastructure, Information, Physical overview and Time elements – or PMESIIPT!

30 Jeremy Bentham's famous efforts to make the English language precise also resulted in serious obfuscation.

31 Much of the attention and resources is devoted to basic (initial) training.

32 Even civilians, including journalists and nongovernmental organization (NGO) representatives, participated in the vetting of a draft of the manual.

33 Sewell, Sarah. "Introduction." *The U. S. Army/Marine Corps Counterinsurgency Field Manual.* University of Chicago Press: Chicago, 2007, p. xxi.

34 The Air Force website says the five most frequently viewed publications are "Aircraft and Equipment Maintenance and Management," "Professional Development Guide," "Officer and Enlisted Evaluation Systems," "Assignments," and "The Tongue and Quill" on oral and written communication. Doctrine is less relevant to the Air Force and perhaps the

Navy, which do not require the smooth coordination of large numbers of enlisted personnel.

35 This is often the case.

36 An independent, nonprofit press.

37 And the military mind too. See a military officer's comic strip "Doctrine Man" on Facebook.

38 In general, training is intended to instill near-automatic responses to specific situations. Education is intended to prepare personnel for the unexpected and to use critical thinking.

4 The military in action

1 Some claim that in certain special cases a bonus of $90,000 was offered.

2 Marine recruiters are evaluated on the basis of the number of their recruits who complete basic training rather than on the number they enlist.

3 In 2009, 3,000 recruiters enlisted about 32,000 enlisted and commissioned fewer than 2,000 officers, just under one each a month. The budget for recruiting was $980 million. Note that "recruitment" primarily applies to enlisted personnel. (Officers are commissioned.) In recent years the Army, which requires the most recruits, is the service that has had the most difficulty meeting its goals. Officers mostly enter service from the Academies or from Reserve Officer Training Corps (ROTC) programs. Some, however, enter through Officer Candidate School (OCS), which involves a twelve-week course. The Air Force program is called Officer Training School (OTS). In each case a college degree is the usual prerequisite.

4 A seventeen-year-old may enlist but only with parental consent.

5 Competition *between* units, though, is encouraged.

6 For 2012 the Army is planning a new Physical Readiness Test and an Army Combat Readiness Test that does take into account future duties.

7 At the Academies many cadets, including women, see this as a double standard and argue that there should be one standard for all. There are different (reduced) standards for older members of the military too. One hears little criticism of these, perhaps because they mostly apply to the higher ranks or because at some point they will apply to anyone still in service.

8 These senior officers are referred to as "fellows" rather than as students.

9 The Army has recently begun a program with New York's Excelsior College that will accept military training and education for up to forty-five credits toward a sixty-credit AA degree. *Army Times*, November 15, 2010, p. 18.

10 Overruns are frequent and large.

11 Remember that one of the unified commands is Transportation. It is the military's unparalleled logistical capacity that draws it into activities, for example, humanitarian relief, that civilians would do if they were provided similar capacity.

12 This also makes the U.S. military expensive.

13 "Analytical Perspectives: Budget of the U. S. Government, Fiscal Year 2010" (www.gpoaccess.gov/usbudget/fy10/pdf/spec.pdf), p. 35.

14 *Army Times*, November 15, 2010, p. 16.

15 Others include units in the Departments of Energy, Treasury, State, and Homeland Security. There is also a Coast Guard unit, which is "military" but reports to Homeland Security rather than the DOD.

16 One source says the DIA has 7,000 employees in one place, and later the same source cites it as having 16,000 employees! One thing to remember about intelligence units is that they not only do not want you to know what they are doing, they are also chary of revealing their budgets and the number of their employees. In recent years DIA has created a covert Human Intelligence Service.

17 One agency does not accept individuals who served in the Peace Corps. Nor can you join the Peace Corps if you have previously been in military intelligence. Also, security clearances are not forever. In some agencies lie detector tests are regularly administered.

18 And also unreliable.

19 Humans, of course, create the computers' programs.

20 One vehicle for this is the Presidential Directive. Often such Directives are secret. Socrates said he who knows he does not know knows. Not true.

21 Secretary of Defense Robert Gates as reported by the *Los Angeles Times*, October 28, 2010. www.globalsecurity.org/intell/library/budget/index. html offers an educated guess as to how that budget is broken down.

22 Photo may be found at www.nsa.gov, accessed March 8, 2011.

23 MNF-I was 80% U.S. troops. The British made a significant contribution, but most of the other country contributions were small, served short rotations, and have been withdrawn. Thus, the U.S. commander was in a good position to manage operations. In World War II working with Allies required the highest level of diplomacy; the major players, the U.S., Britain and the Soviet Union, had diverse interests. In addition, there were numerous other players including troops from throughout the British Empire.

24 In the early 1990s public pressure forced the United States to leave its Clark Air Base and its Subic Bay Naval Air Station in the Philippines. U.S. Special Operations forces are, however, currently engaged in antiterrorism operations there.

25 These states may have National Guard installations. Note: the Coast Guard has three locations in landlocked West Virginia.

26 The DOD Base Structure Report, which is a portfolio of real property (2010 Baseline), describes a footprint in all fifty states and thirty-eight foreign locations. Only twenty overseas sites are listed as "large," i.e. valued at $1.71 billion or more; twelve are listed as "medium" or from $915 million to $1.71 billion.

27 Some military-like covert missions are conducted by the CIA but in recent years the military's Special Forces have been expanded and given more "direct action."

28 Johnson, Chalmers. Nemesis: *The Last Days of the American Republic*. New York: Metropolitan Books, 2006, p. 5.
29 Forward presence in Europe was primarily directed toward the Soviet Union, and in Japan and South Korea against North Korea and China. Recently a presence has developed versus Iran. What we see as a presence may feel to others like a threat.
30 Also some U.S. authorities believed that asking soldiers to participate in peacekeeping would make them ineffective as warriors.
31 "Anti" is defensive; "counter" is offensive.
32 The military is not necessarily enthusiastic about its many non-war missions.

5 Weapons and capabilities

1 Some believe that there were once more than 60,000 or 70,000 nuclear weapons between the two adversaries.
2 Others are in storage and may be slated for dismantling.
3 Although the United States has custody of these weapons, European nationals are trained and prepared to use them. www.plowshares.org/news-analysis/world-nuclear-stockpile-report, accessed October 21, 2011.
4 The Army's tactical nukes are another issue.
5 The United States has replaced Multiple Independently Targetable Re-entry Vehicles (MIRVs) with single warheads on these missiles.
6 *Air Force Magazine* publishes an annual USAF Almanac, "The Air Force in Facts and Figures." The 2010 issue is used here.
7 Also known as Remotely Piloted Vehicles (RPVs).
8 Sometimes called "the Viper."
9 An even newer F-35 Lightning is being tested.
10 Note that aircraft have an alphanumeric designation. The letters stand for function, thus "A" is for attack aircraft, "B" for bomber, "C" for transport/cargo, "E" for electronics, "F" for fighter, "H" for helicopter, "K" for tanker, "M" for special operations, and "T" for trainer. The number specifies the particular kind of plane.
11 CIA UAVs, their missions, and their accomplishments are not part of the public record/discourse.
12 Some experts consider the Russian Kalashnikov or AK-47 as the most reliable all-around rifle. It is low cost and the most widely used rifle.
13 TOW stands for tube-launched, optically tracked, wired data link, guided missile.
14 The larger the ticket item, the larger the variation in price estimates from different sources. Also, items continually are improved, so an Apache might be considered a whole class of aircraft just as a Honda includes a number of variations. I am doing my best.

15 Nevertheless its battle fleet tonnage is larger than that of the next thirteen countries combined – and most of those are allies. Still, there is some concern about China's current naval buildup.
16 PBS has an excellent documentary, "Carrier."
17 No, Virginia, there is no longer such a thing as a battleship.
18 Note the Marine creed in Chapter 2.

6 The budget

1 Much of the discussion in this chapter is drawn from Michael E. O'Hanlon's *The Science of War* published by Princeton University Press in 2009. The second basic source for information is www.budget.mil.
2 This does not include expenses related to nuclear weapons included in the Department of Energy budget, Treasury Department payments for military pensions, or the Veterans Affairs budget.
3 Foreign operations encompasses a wide range of expenditures on things such as HIV/AIDS, food assistance, initiatives to combat transnational crime, and support for basic education. These are implemented by a variety of agencies and departments including DOD.
4 See www.state.gov/r/pa/prs/ps/2009/05/123160.htm, accessed October 21, 2011, and www.dhs.gov/ynews/releases/pr_1241715252729.shtm, accessed October 21, 2011.
5 Update: the DOD request for 2011 totaled $712,000,000,000. This included a base of $549,000,000,000 and $159,000,000,000 for the Iraq and Afghanistan wars. If all defense-related items from all agencies were included the total would be $861,000,000,000, 22 percent of the total federal budget according to the Center for Strategic and Budgetary Assessments. http://www/csbaonline.org/publications/2010/06/fy-2011-defense-budget-analysis/, accessed October 21, 2011.
6 There are about 1,400,000 active duty military and more than 800,000 in the Guard and Reserves. The DOD also employs more than 700,000 civilians. Possibly as many as another 700,000 work in industries supported by DOD spending.
7 The Korean War is estimated at $480 billion, Vietnam at $680 billion, and Desert Storm at $90 billion, *but* more than 90 percent of Desert Storm costs were paid by allies.
8 Waging war far from home is very expensive.
9 Note that the continents of Africa and Latin America escape mention, although the United States now has an African Combat Command and there is some action in Latin America.
10 U.S. Navy tonnage has shrunk since the end of the Cold War, but has it shrunk as much as would be sensible? Its battle fleet remains larger than that of the next thirteen countries combined – and eleven of those thirteen

are U.S. allies or partners. See Secretary of Defense Robert Gates's April 2009 speech "A Balanced Strategy" (www.defense.gov/speeches/speech. aspx?speechid=1346, accessed October 21, 2011).

11 Military planners even have plans for contingencies which go beyond formal, public, U.S. commitments such as plans for stabilizing Kashmir, clearing the Indonesian Straits, and securing Nigerian oil.

12 Overseas bases have a variety of purposes. These include ground combat bases including bases with a deterrence mission, ports for ships, bases for tactical aircraft, and logistics hubs. Currently about 220,000 troops are stationed at sea or abroad, *not* including troops in Iraq and Afghanistan.

13 Discretionary? The Congress tends to treat it more as obligatory. That is, when there is discussion about cutting the federal budget, the defense budget has often been considered exempt by many legislators both Republicans and Democrats.

14 As noted above, these documents are often neither specific nor timely.

15 The DOD expects the services to speak with one voice, DOD's voice, on budget items.

16 In the 1930s there was a contrary effort to prevent contractors from making any profit at all from war or preparations for it.

17 Private military companies (PMCs) experienced a boom in the 1990s and are used by a number of countries and private organizations around the globe.

18 The United Nations 1989 Convention on Mercenaries generally forbids their use. The United States has not signed this Convention.

19 The name change came after bad publicity about what many saw as an excessive use of force by Blackwater security personnel.

20 The Defense Security Cooperation Agency (DSCA) administers these sales. It provides a detailed account of agreements and deliveries on line.

21 In addition, in 2009 the International Military Training and Education (IMET) Program received over $530,000,000 and trained as many as 70,000 individuals according to a report jointly issued by the State and Defense Departments.

22 A 2010 Congressional Research Service report titled "U. S. Arms Sales: Agreements with and Deliveries to Major Clients, 2002–2009" provides a great deal of data.

23 It is complicated. After recognizing China in 1971, in 1979 the United States passed the Taiwan Relations Act setting up something like an embassy there. The act provided for arms sales of a "defensive nature" and noted that any attempt to change the status of Taiwan by other than peaceful means would be of "grave concern."

24 *Financial Times*, September, 27, 2010.

25 *Wall Street Journal*, September 12, 2010. For the United States, diplomacy and profits are not the only issues. There are numerous jobs associated with military sales and there are now competitors for such sales in Western Europe and also in Russia.

7 Policy questions

1 Only the United States and Somalia have not ratified the last convention.
2 It should be noted that the United States may honor conventions that it has not ratified.
3 This was not true in World War II. Some members of Congress even resigned to enlist. At least since the Vietnam War the top economic echelon has been underrepresented.
4 Senior officers may retire by age fifty. They are educated, experienced, and fit and most are eager for a continued active life. Their talents should not be wasted.

8 Some resources for more information

1 For example the Chief of Staff of the Air Force's Professional Reading Program for 2011 lists fourteen books in three categories: leadership, strategic context, and military heritage.

Index

Notes: As the subject of this book is the U.S. Military, entries under military and United States of America have been kept to a minimum. Readers are advised to look for more specific terms.